ASHLEY,

THANKS FOR

BEING SUCH A

GREAT PARTNER!

no goob.

Jeff

THE 5-DAY TURNAROUND

"It's a challenge for legacy companies to stay relevant. The market keeps changing. *The 5-Day Turnaround* offers actionable ways for leaders to create transformative change by sharing their vision and keeping their people at the center of the process."

PAUL BROWN, *CEO, Inspire Brands*

"*The 5-Day Turnaround* is a practical and inspiring business book. The narrative and tips it offers will help leaders build trust and involve their people as they work to do things differently for the good of the company."

HALA MODDELMOG, *CEO & President, Metro Atlanta Chamber, and former CEO & President, Susan G. Komen for the Cure*

"Jeff personifies the definition of entrepreneur: resourceful, ambitious, and full of grit. Transforming established corporations to act more entrepreneurial requires these attributes in spades, and no one is better to expand on them than Jeff. The only established corporations that thrive tomorrow are the ones that are more entrepreneurial today. Unlock growth by following the strategies laid out in *The 5-Day Turnaround* and ensure continued success."

DAVID CUMMINGS, *Founder of Pardot & Atlanta Tech Village*

"Jeff's book will help leaders everywhere refocus on the most important things, like values and how we treat each other—and thereby unlock higher levels of success, satisfaction, and even happiness!"

CHARLES BREWER, *CEO & Founder, Mindspring*

"As a successful business leader, Jeff has mastered the art of the startup. Now you can too. Whether your company is large or small, this book is filled with hacks and tips to help you and your team succeed. If you are a leader looking for ways to ignite growth quickly, this book is for you!"

ERIC LENT, *SVP, Global Marketing, InterContinental Hotels Group*

"I've spent the better part of my career in big corporations, and I can tell you this—innovation doesn't just happen. It's tricky and sensitive, but when it works, it is like jet fuel for the organization. Jeff shares a startup mindset that he's proven through the process of successfully growing multiple companies from idea to market leading. This book is required reading."

MOLLY BATTIN, *Chief Corporate Marketing and Brand Strategy Officer, WarnerMedia*

"Engaging, fun, smart, and highly impactful. Just a few words I use to describe Jeff Hilimire, but also his new book, *The 5-Day Turnaround*. The stories and lessons roll off the pages and are a quick read based on the relatable storytelling format. Embedded throughout is Jeff's clear approach to business, collaboration, and the importance of a well-defined Purpose, Vision, Tenets, and Values (PVTV)—the catalyst to business success. The lessons and action steps provided throughout *The 5-Day Turnaround* are incredibly actionable. I highly recommend this book for agency leaders, perennial and new entrepreneurs, or corporate leaders championing change."

MARK M. O'BRIEN, *CEO & President, LakePoint Sports*

"Leading organizations and teams to achieve great results takes inspired and passionate leadership. This book will help unlock that passion within you!"

DR. VALERIE MONTGOMERY RICE, *President & Dean, Morehouse School of Medicine*

THE 5-DAY TURNA ROUND

Be the leader you always wanted to be.

JEFF HILIMIRE

First printing 2019

Book design by Michael Stanley and Najdan Mancic

ISBN 978-1-7338689-0-7

Published by Ripples of Hope Publishing
www.5dayturnaround.com

"Only those who dare to fail greatly can ever achieve greatly."

—*Robert F. Kennedy*

DEDICATION

This book is dedicated to my wife, Emily, who I've been in love with since we were 16-year-olds. You are my everything.

And to our little startup at home—Zac, Drew, Kaitlyn, Hannah, and Kai—who bring me more joy than any one person deserves. I love you all.

CONTENTS

Stan Rapp is the retired founder and CEO of the RAPP agency, which grew into a $600-million global enterprise. His Foreword sets the stage for *The 5-Day Turnaround*—what he describes as a fun-to-read learning experience. Rapp was named by *Advertising Age* magazine as one of the "101 stars who shaped the history of advertising in the 20th century." He is the author of seven books, first predicting and then tracking the transition to one-to-one marketing. Rapp was recently chosen for the Marketing Legend award by the business school of UT Dallas. His Foreword is an insightful introduction to the story you are about to read.

Meet Will, the CEO of a marketing agency. He turns a bold campaign pitch into an opportunity to help his former colleague and long-time friend, Matt, transform a large and sluggish corporate department into a nimble organization.

Vision Casting / Confidence / Quick Wins / Internal Support / Putting It All Together

The *Do or Die Mindset* focuses on how you think and position your team to make decisions, act, and thrive within the organization and the marketplace. Gaining this confidence takes an unflinching belief in yourself, fearlessness, and a clear understanding of how your work produces results.

The Do or Die Mindset / Becoming Fearless / Worst-Case Scenarios / Becoming Results-Oriented / The Environment / Meeting Times / Reputation Management

Documenting your PVTV (Purpose, Vision, Tenets, and Values) is the first step toward team alignment. You'll consider why the company and your team exists, what type of team you need to become, and how to achieve transformation.

Crafting Your Purpose, Vision, Tenets, Values / Team Responsibility & Personal Responsibility / Morning Rituals / Headspace / Finding Your People

Knowing your team members and how they fit into the Vision for your department is critical to creating a culture of recognizing wins, instilling PVTV, and aligning people around those shared goals.

Words Matter / Aligning People / Right People, Right Position, Right Time / Trust / Titles

A leader's ability to react quickly to take advantage of business opportunities is based on the capacity to keep focus, lead by example, embrace a minimally viable product (MVP) approach, and remove stumbling blocks to progress.

Productivity at a Glance / The One Thing / Leading by Example / Idea Killers / Client Relationships

Failure is a part of the growth process. Leaders can use purposeful failure as stepping stones to accomplish real change and build a platform for progress. Conclude the journey by understanding the causes of failure and what steps to take to learn from them.

Taking Chances / Welcoming Failure / Setting Goals / Growth Outcomes

Acting like a successful startup begins with you—the leader thinking like the CEO of a startup. Embrace the Do or Die Mindset, have an unflinching belief in yourself, act fearlessly, and be results-oriented. Define and live the PVTV for your team and operationalize it. Make sure you have the right people in the right places and trust in them. If your team trusts you, they will take your direction and align around the PVTV. Then you can work with speed—as long as you stay focused and manage work time well.

In the Appendix, you'll find resources to help you think through all of these critical steps and exercises you can perform with your team to accomplish your own Five-Day Turnaround.

Put the insights from Will's Five-Day Turnaround to practice in your own business. This workbook follows along with the day-by-day structure of the story, offering personal reflection questions and actionable exercises you can share with your team.

BUSINESS & LIFE HACKS....................222

A number of key considerations and actions are mentioned throughout the book. Access them all in a compiled section here.

BONUS SECTION....................233

Visit *The 5-Day Turnaround* website (www.5dayturnaround.com/bonus) for a bonus section that details a conversation between Will and Matt about optimizing the productivity and cost of team meetings, complete with useful hacks you can implement immediately in your own team space.

Be sure to check out this same section of the website to read a bonus chapter, "Friendly People," that offers additional insights into ways to create a company culture that keeps teams focused, motivated, and inspired.

FOREWORD

My favorite learning experience still happens inside a book. Whatever the format—e-book, audiobook, or print—intriguing content takes me to places and thoughts I have never experienced before. Your selection of *The 5-Day Turnaround* tells me you share that joy.

Even as digital has so profoundly changed publishing, very little is different in how books are conceived and written. This sameness is especially true of most business books—whatever guidance the author advocates becomes the source of the content.

Sometimes, however, the experience is distinct. The business book you're about to read is a fascinating story about two fictional protagonists who make important changes in how they lead and in the organizations they manage.

I'm reminded of Michelle Obama's comment, "Even if a book takes on serious topics, it should still be fun to read." (She certainly ought to know. Her bestseller sold two million copies in the first 15 days.)

The 5-Day Turnaround is the fun-to-read story of a team leader who evolves the stodgy culture at a longstanding business enterprise into a hotbed of entrepreneurial thinking. The transformation carries out over five meetings—just five days. The seemingly impossible pace of change makes for a dramatic tale. The real-life scenario provides an exceptional learning experience.

o﹏o

I have known Jeff Hilimire for close to 20 years. My admiration for him knows no bounds. He has embarked on and succeeded in a series of impressive journeys—some at the very same time—all driven by his passionate commitment to making an out-sized, positive impact on the world.

Jeff's course to becoming a successful serial entrepreneur began in 1998 in a dorm room at UNC-Charlotte, where he launched Spunlogic, his first of four ventures. The digital ad agency thrived in the turbulent early years of the 21st century and within a decade was working with an array of famous brands.

He sold Spunlogic and launched his second prosperous venture, Engauge. The digital marketing agency provided advertising and digital services to leading Fortune 500 companies. After less than a decade, he negotiated the sale of the company to Publicis Group, one of the most significant creative communications groups in the world.

One of the first to spot the potential of the smartphone to usher in an era of mobile marketing, Jeff went again to his entrepreneurial roots to launch his third startup. Dragon Army became the first of its kind to focus entirely on creating unique mobile experiences for major brands.

In the midst of his own tremendous business journey, Jeff also has been a mentor at several startup incubators and has overseen the growth of one of the fastest-growing nonprofits in Atlanta.

If you are one of the thousands of readers of Jeff's long-running blog, *Begin the Begin*, you know that the masthead says it's about entrepreneurship, leadership, and doing good.

Jeff's "doing good" journey began earnestly in 2015. This was the year when he launched a fourth enterprise—this one a nonprofit called 48in48. Jeff and his co-founder Adam Walker, the CEO of Sideways8, brought together marketing and technology volunteers for 48 hours to build 48 websites for 48 local nonprofits.

Here is how Jeff describes the progress.

"In October of 2015, 150 people showed up at Ponce City Market in Atlanta for our first attempt at building 48 nonprofit websites in 48 hours (with Delta Air Lines as our founding partner).

"The first event went so well, we decided to try a new market and took 48in48 to New York City in 2016, while also hosting our second Atlanta event over the same weekend.

"After successfully pulling off those events, our big idea was born—to host 48 events in 48 cities around the world *on the same weekend* by 2025. This endeavour will impact more than 2,000 nonprofits, engage over 10,000 skilled volunteers, and produce greater than $75 million in charity hours to help make the world a better place. We are on track to turn our ambition into a reality."

Quite a journey! The numbers speak to impact. Between 2015 and 2018, 48in48 served more than 700 nonprofits worldwide, with $1.5 million in services donated at each event.

Jeff has an amazing odyssey of business and nonprofit startup successes. He has a third as well, which is reflected directly in this book. He is intently looking at ways to make learning easier for the next generation of business managers and nonprofit leaders. The pace of change in a post-digital economy creates a lifetime need for constant learning. Jeff is striving for new and better ways to make that happen.

Writing *The 5-Day Turnaround* as a captivating story, rather than a traditional business book, is one of his most promising initiatives.

The characters in the story resemble people you encounter on the job every day. The two protagonists, Matt and Will, worked together at a thriving startup. When that business was acquired, they went their separate ways. A decade later, Will is a successful entrepreneur with a respected ad agency. Matt is a corporate team leader at a Fortune 1000 company.

As the story opens, Matt has invited Will—along with three other agencies—to bid for the corporation's advertising assignment. What the two long-time colleagues and friends discover, though, is that Matt is frustrated and saddled by his company's play-it-safe culture. Will brings a call for startup boldness and a plan to make it happen—in five short meetings.

Does Will succeed in the pitch?

Can Matt and Will confront issues more substantial than a new product kick-off campaign?

What will you glean from the narrative to boost your own leadership?

Sit back and enjoy how Matt tries to achieve what looks impossible—infusing startup audacity at his play-it-safe company.

And so the journey begins.

Stan Rapp
April 2019

PRELUDE

"And that's our pitch. We'd love to know what you think!"

Silence.

To be honest, I had expected a bit of post-pitch silence. Our team at the agency had worked long hours over the past three months to give Matt and his team a significant amount to consider.

After reaching a few dead-ends, we came up with a big idea—an approach with the potential to disrupt an entire industry. It was one of the most promising business solutions we'd ever created at my agency. I couldn't wait to hear Matt's reaction.

Asking a prospect to break new ground is always risky. One thing I've learned is you never know how your audience will react to a truly daring concept. During the pitch, I was aware of Matt's body language and, at times, felt he was getting it. At other moments, he seemed lost in thought.

Was it indecision I was sensing?

When we worked side by side at Crackersnap Tech in the past, Matt and I were a great duo. We were even known to finish each other's sentences on occasion. Right now, that all seemed a long time ago.

"Excellent!" Matt exclaimed, breaking my train of thought. "We asked you to push us, to really challenge us. Speaking for everyone here, I can say you did just that."

The rest of his team, including those who were less attentive earlier, nodded their heads. The one exception was the newest member, a woman named Meredith. From the start of the pitch to the finish, she took notes continuously, which is generally a positive sign.

"Thanks!" I responded to Matt. "Do you have any questions for us? We can walk you through the timeline if you like. Building a new approach to target buyers is something we would do with your technology team—"

Matt cut me off.

"Actually, I think we're good on the details for now. We really appreciate your team spending so much time on this one. As you know, today was the last of the presentations we've scheduled. Now the work begins on our side before we can make a decision. Thanks again for coming."

Matt's polite words were not the enthusiastic response my team had hoped to hear.

He stood up to leave, and we all followed.

As my associates packed the display boards and made small talk, I made my way over to where Matt was standing.

"So, are we still on for coffee tomorrow morning?" I asked.

"You bet. It gives me a chance to bring you up to speed on the process we'll follow the rest of the way. Excellent stuff today, Will. You sure were in top form."

We said our goodbyes, yet I had the feeling he was holding something back. Once in the elevator, our team congratulated one another on a job well done. I could sense their relief that the pitch was behind us. Mostly, I was looking ahead to my first good night's sleep in a while.

Matt and I first met when we both worked at Crackersnap Tech, an artificial intelligence and technology startup. He reported directly to the CMO, and I was in charge of sales. We left soon after Crackersnap was acquired by a big conglomerate ten years ago.

He moved on to become CMO of Titan, a Fortune 1000 company. I went on to become a VP at Ideathon, a highly regarded problem-solving consultancy. After four years spent mostly setting stalled companies on a new path, it felt right to risk being an entrepreneur with my own startup. Now, I'm running a thriving, six-year-old digital ad agency. Things are going well. We've grown to just under 100 employees and have gained some impressive clients. Winning Titan would bring us our largest account so far.

Who would have thought back then that pitching to be Matt's Agency of Record would be part of our future?

Matt and I did a good job of staying in touch after leaving Crackersnap. Luckily, our current business offices are only a ten-minute Lyft ride apart. We keep up with each other by getting together now and then at The Steaming Cup—our favorite local coffee spot.

Matt's move up the corporate ladder was no surprise. I always saw him as a person with impressive talents, including a mix of creative ideas and a down-to-earth knack for getting the job done.

I was eager to hear what Matt thought of our pitch. Drifting off to sleep that night, it was tough deciding which was more likely—a thumbs-up or a thumbs-down.

As usual, I was at The Steaming Cup in the morning well before Matt. It's my habit, when meeting someone, to get there early for some undisturbed email time. Matt, as was his custom, strolled in at 8 a.m., exactly as we had agreed.

"Over here!" I waved to Matt. "The line was getting long, so I grabbed your usual black coffee. Don't worry. I won't put it on your first invoice."

Matt laughed nervously. The obvious reference to the pitch made him uncomfortable. My attempt at humor was something I regretted almost at once.

What struck me as we started sipping our coffee was how much older Matt seemed to be. It was as if the last few years had taken quite a toll.

"So, busy week?" I asked, restarting the conversation.

"Yeah, always. But busy is good, right? I gotta say, though, I've never felt so underwater. Even after adding two team members, it's hard to keep up. Things change so fast these days!

"And the pitch process to land an agency was a pain—no offense to you guys. You did great. It's some of the others we've seen. The repeated briefings. All those requests for more data. The maneuvering to get an edge. The endless presentations to sit through. I never knew there were so many different lines of attack an agency can come up with and still end up in the same place," he complained.

"It's rough on the agencies as well. We work our tails off for weeks, and at best we have a 30% chance of winning. That's the industry average."

Matt looked up from his coffee. "Really? Those seem like tough odds."

"Yep, nature of the beast. If I had known how tough it was to win new clients, I might have chucked the whole agency gambit."

I quickly corrected myself. "No, that's not true. The process of solving problems with new ideas is so exciting. Also, there are lots of great people to work with on both the agency side and the client side."

Matt shook his head. "Huh, sounds like the old Crackersnap days…and the complete opposite of what it's like at Titan."

What came next is what I dreaded hearing.

"Which is why I don't think we can choose your agency to work with us on this project."

"Oh," I said, with a sick feeling at the pit of my stomach. "Well, I sure did appreciate the chance to pitch. Sometimes we nail it, and sometimes we don't. I get that."

"No, Will. Actually, your take on the challenge we're facing is perfect. Seriously, it's the kind of thinking we need to outdo those newcomers eating our lunch. My team admires what you came up with," he reassured me.

Matt stood up and walked over to the counter for a coffee refill. I stayed at the table, coming to terms with what he just said.

"Gotta say, I just don't get it," I started right off when he rejoined me. "With all those positives, why didn't you choose us? Is it the price? We can look at the scope. I know we were a little over your budget, but we can work on that."

"Nope, your budget was fine, no worries there. Several other estimates were higher than yours. Honestly, the reason we can't work with you is—and I really hate to admit this—we could never pull it off. It's not doable for a team with our limitations."

I pressed for a better answer. "Meaning what exactly?"

"Look, the reality is we're like every other established business. We spend most of our time in meetings. When we try to implement anything to break the mold, we over-complicate and over-process it. During the years I've been here, the number of times we went 'all out' in a genuinely new direction comes down to zero. I've learned to settle for marginal gains we can make work."

He had trouble meeting my eyes. I guessed he was embarrassed by what he was saying.

"But at Crackersnap you were the champion of reaching for the stars despite the risks!" I exclaimed.

"Titan isn't Crackersnap, Will. And we're not unique. I have friends at other large companies that have been around forever, and they struggle with the same constraints. Put simply, they don't know how to move with the speed of a startup. That's why up-and-coming entrepreneurs are kicking our butts. You should know, some of the winners are your clients!"

He was right. My agency works with both established brands and hot new startups. As you'd expect, the startups move much faster than the big guys. In fact, sometimes they go so fast we have a hard time keeping up with them.

Rather than respond to Matt, I decided to get my own coffee refill. What I needed was a few minutes to think through a wild idea that had just crossed my mind.

Maybe losing the pitch was not a done deal.

What if I could help Matt turn around his situation to become more like the startup where he once thrived? If that happened, he'd be able to work with our agency after all. What was racing through my head was all those CMOs I put on the right track when working at Ideathon.

Coming back to the table, I fired a question at Matt. "Did you mean it when you said your team loved our approach, but you lack confidence in them pulling it off?"

Matt came back with, "On one hand, your proposal outclasses anything else we've seen. On the other hand, with the culture at Titan, we could never make it happen."

"Matt, please excuse my being blunt, but walking away from a marvelous opportunity is not the you I remember."

I continued, gaining strength. "Do you recall how we had to overcome stumbling blocks at Crackersnap each time the company's growth stalled?"

"Sure do. Sorting out the real problem worked every time. Once we identified the actual hurdle, a solution began to take shape," he agreed.

"Matt, you're facing a similar challenge now. Backing away from taking bold action at Titan keeps your team from doing their best. The answer is to bring about a sea change that allows you to be the leader you truly are."

Suddenly curious, Matt asked, "What are you getting at?"

"Why not hold off on making your agency selection for another month or so," I proposed. "During that time, maybe we can get together one day a week to figure out how your team at Titan can act more like a successful startup. Overall, it would take just five days of your time." I paused. "Are you with me so far?"

"Will, is there something in your coffee? This sounds a bit…"

"Crazy?" I said, finishing his sentence, just like in the early days of our partnership. "Trust me. Everything I saw about turning thinking around while running Ideathon meetings tells me we can pull this off. All I'm asking for is one month's delay in choosing an agency. That still leaves time for you to go with any shop you want if what we proposed yesterday still doesn't seem actionable. All your options remain open."

I waited a few seconds and then pushed to close the deal. "What do you say?"

Matt looked at me, squinting his eyes a bit, deep in thought. He took a long drink of coffee, set the cup down, and asked, "Do you honestly think it's possible to change Titan in our five days together?"

My answer brought a smile to his face. "You bet I do! Remember, we are not trying to change all of Titan just yet. This step is about evolving how your team gets things done. We turned around more formidable situations at Crackersnap in less face-to-face time. To change your team's behavior, you've got to make the first move. With your revamped leadership, they can do a u-turn in far less time than you think."

"I have to admit I'm intrigued," Matt said. "And there is room in the schedule for a delay in making my agency choice." He was doing the math in his head, his fingers tapping as he made the calculations.

Matt looked straight at me and said, "Will, I need to weigh the pros and cons. What I can agree to for now is an answer, one way or the other, in a phone call tomorrow evening. Is that okay with you?"

"Absolutely," I said. "Just call my cell."

"Perfect," Matt responded.

We shook hands and spoke our goodbyes. Matt headed for the parking lot, and I fired up the Lyft app to request a ride.

Tomorrow, I would know the answer. If Matt went for The Five-Day Turnaround, my agency would still have a chance to win the account. What had just happened at The Steaming Cup left my heart pounding.

A glance at my Apple Watch showed there was still time to get to my first meeting of the day.

While riding to my client, SalesLive, I was sorting out next steps should we get the go-ahead in tomorrow's phone call. The toughest part would be staying in sync with Titan norms while bringing about a flip-flop in the culture of Matt's team.

Thinking about what we would encounter, I recalled a comment my mentor Charles had made recently. "You know when companies first start out, they're trying to do what has never seen the light of day before. If success follows, all the energy and passion they put into making the early days a triumph shifts to protecting what they built. Soon the company's growth slows down, and further progress is minimal. It's the trap every established company faces."

Something I hadn't shared with Matt was that Charles and I have been collaborating on an article for *Harvard Business Review* about the many ways the mindset at startups and grown-up businesses differ. Charles is a generation older and a brilliant entrepreneur. Our joint research has identified the top traits of successful startups. Lately, we've been exploring how those traits might be adapted to unlock growth at companies that have left their startup culture far behind.

My mind was buzzing with how my talks with Charles could be used to support Matt's about-face.

I turned into the parking lot and focus quickly shifted to my meeting with Shera, the CEO of SalesLive. She personified the very traits I admire in successful startups. Maybe Shera being my first contact after the morning chat with Matt would prove to be a good omen.

◦⌐◦

The first thing you notice when you enter SalesLive is Shera's imprint on everything.

Her startup had just passed the 200-employee benchmark, after only three years in business. Immediately, I'm struck by the massive flat screen monitor on the wall behind the receptionist rotating between three screens:

Our Vision

To eliminate the tension between
salespeople and their prospects

Our Core Values

All for one and one for all
Taking advantage is out, gaining advantage is in
Always two steps ahead

Our Metrics

New Customers This Quarter: 52
Revenue This Quarter: $5,632,282 (11% above goal)
Customer Churn: 4%

"Will!" I heard Shera shout as she came my way. "Great to see you! How do you like our new space?"

After a quick hug—Shera does everything *quickly*!—I said, "Fantastic. Still find it hard to take in how fast you've scaled your business!"

"Oh, does it seem that way? I suppose it would if you look at us from the outside. SalesLive is a very different company from the one we started. We took a few swings at bat before getting where we wanted to be. Pivoting is part of the growth process after all, right?" she said.

My agency had worked with Shera for the past two years, and in that time we had helped her rebrand twice. Her ability to successfully pivot SalesLive's direction when she hit a roadblock was impressive.

As Shera showed me around the office, I noticed the motivational posters on the walls. They reminded me of the startup culture she encourages.

Never want to be criticized?
Never be different.

We have a strategic plan.
It's called getting there first.

If opportunity doesn't knock,
build a door.

As I paused and read each of these, Shera noted my interest. "You know, those are great, but they're really for our guests."

"What do you mean?" I asked.

"Well, the messages on the posters are embedded in our culture. They aren't sayings that we need to remind ourselves about," she said. "I mostly have these for when customers and friends come over. Gives them a picture to snap with their phones."

There was a wink with that last bit, and I quickly put my phone back in my pocket.

Shera added, "If you have to put these posters up to remind your people how to act, it's probably too late."

Fair enough, I thought.

She led me into a conference room with a huge whiteboard serving as one wall and a large monitor on the opposite side. Conference phones were on both ends of the table. There were several bowls of high-end, healthy snacks for munching.

We settled into our seats. Shera filled me in on the latest news about her upcoming new product launch. We exchanged some early stage ideas about specific campaign options.

When everything on the agenda was answered, I asked if she had 30 minutes for something I wanted to run by her.

"Shoot," she said, standing up and reaching out to grab a nutrition bar.

"You worked in corporate America before starting your own business. Is that right?" I asked, knowing what the answer would be. Shera had been a highly regarded leader at a Fortune 1000 company.

"Oh yeah, I was Ms. Corporate America before starting SalesLive. I worked at Burwire Industries for nine years. Climbed the corporate ladder to VP of Operations."

"And remind me, what caused your leap to start SalesLive?"

She smiled. "Honestly, I got tired of the constant feeling we were moving too slow. That was part of it. Mostly I got tired of not being able to create a culture of my own. I had promising ideas but usually couldn't test them out. My boss had a boss, and he answered to a board, which answered to Wall Street. I guess I wanted to see what I could do if it were all up to me—and the best people I could recruit, of course. And then there was the radical concept keeping me awake nights that now inspires SalesLive. I thought it could never be brought to life at Burwire."

"And do you have that here, the ability to move in any direction you want?" I asked.

"Yep, and it's a great feeling!" she said emphatically. Shera was pacing back and forth and becoming more animated.

She had made her point, but I felt she was overlooking something.

"You have investors, right? And an official board?" I asked.

"Yep, they're great. A few from here and a couple from the Valley," she explained.

"Don't they have a say in what you do?" I asked.

"Well, sure, I guess. I have to get their approval before I acquire a new company, or move to new office space, or spend more than a certain amount." She was looking up toward the ceiling and thinking now. "And hiring key executives, I have to run that by them as well. So yeah, they have some control, but for the day-to-day, the buck stops here."

"Gotcha," I said. "And what about customers? I know in my business I sometimes feel like I work for them!"

She laughed. "That's true. Customers can be kind of demanding sometimes. We recently had to restructure our entire Customer Success Team because of the way one customer wanted to start using our platform."

"And what about your partners? I know your platform ties directly into Salesforce and LinkedIn. How are they to work with?" I asked.

"They're okay, but some of our software partners make it tough to meet deadlines."

"So," I summed up. "You're able to do what you want with your company, as long as your investors, your board, your customers, and your partners all agree with it. Does that sound about right?"

She squinted her eyes and looked at me, clearly wondering where I was going with this. "Mmmm hmmm…And…?"

"Let me ask you this final question," I said. "Do you think there's a chance that you could have done more at Burwire, but your mindset was that it wasn't your company, so you had to defer to corporate roadblocks?

"In reality, no one is entirely free to make a unilateral decision without being sure it works for various stakeholders. Even, it would seem, entrepreneurs," I added.

"Ah, I see what you did there," she smiled. "I'd have to think about it some more, but for now I can agree. You're saying it's more about the mindset I was in at that time. Maybe if I had my entrepreneur hat on while at Burwire, I might have accomplished more than I thought was possible."

"Right. Or at least that's what I'm wondering," I said. This idea that someone who isn't an entrepreneur could act like one at an established company was what Charles and I had spent a great deal of time examining. Soon I would be bringing the concept to life in my training sessions with Matt.

"Hey, you still with me over there?" Shera asked. I realized I had been deep in thought and hadn't notice that she was up at the whiteboard.

"Sorry, I was just thinking that this sounds good in theory but wondering if it would work in practice."

"Exactly! So, what is needed to make it happen? I think I can picture it." With her usual positive take on a challenge, Shera began to draw on the whiteboard. She outlined three intersecting circles and wrote the word "Confidence" in one of them.

"Seems to me that no matter what, if a person were going to be entrepreneurial in a corporate setting, they'd need a great amount of self-confidence. That was probably the biggest thing holding me back at Burwire. I wasn't confident enough to buck the system."

Before I could comment, she moved on to another one of the interlocking circles and wrote the words "Internal Support/ Politics." She paused over the word "Politics," erased it, shook her head, and then wrote it larger again.

"You must have solid relationships internally, particularly with senior leadership. I don't think anyone can create change within an organization if they haven't done the hard work of earning respect from the right people beforehand," she said.

"I notice you wrote and rewrote 'politics,' how come?" I asked.

She nodded. "I hate what the word stands for within a company. Politics to me means someone putting their career ahead of the company's goals. It usually means making others look bad in order to prop yourself up. At SalesLive, we sniff out the first sign of politics, and we crush it!" With this, she opened her hand in the air and closed it quickly in a fist.

"But," she continued. "A leader within a sizable company does have to play the game a little to be successful. You have to know whose opinion matters and how to gain allies if you want to do big things."

"I buy that," I said.

She went back to the whiteboard and looked at the third circle. She put the end of the marker in her mouth, deep in thought. She then nodded and wrote, "Quick wins."

"Yep, that's it. You need someone with tremendous confidence, and that person needs to have close internal relationships as well as the ability to get some quick wins," she said.

"Quick wins. That makes sense," I said. "If your first effort is a swing for the fences and you strike out, that could be it for you. But if you show some progress, and build momentum slowly, then you'll be able to have more success as you go."

"Right!" she exclaimed. "At least that's where I'd start. By the way, why the questions?"

At that moment a young man poked his head in the door. "Shera, your 2 p.m. is here."

"Thanks, Jeremy, I'll be right there," she said. I knew our time was over.

"Thanks for your time, Shera. How much do you charge per hour?" I joked.

"You can't afford my services anymore, Will," she joked back. "But good luck with whatever you're working on!" Another quick hug and she was out the door.

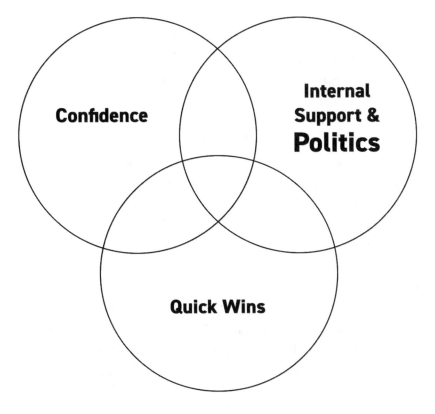

Sitting alone in the conference room, I looked up at what she had written on the whiteboard.

The first thing I'd need to do with Matt is to convince him that the mindset he enjoyed at Crackersnap could be brought back to life at Titan. Before that could happen, tomorrow's phone call would have to go well.

I arrived at work early the next morning, eager to get the day rolling. I like the relatively quiet time in the office before everyone starts shuffling in.

This particular morning, I arrived at 7:15 a.m. and a couple of people were already at the office. Both were client services team members, meaning they interface with our clients to ensure our projects are successful.

I walked past them, waved and said good morning, and then turned the corner into the heart of our office. We had moved into this space last year, and I still loved the way we had organized it. We had worked with a local architecture firm to make sure we got just the right feel.

To say our office is an open environment would be an understatement. While we do have cubes, they are low-walled and set up in pods of four. Each pod shares a common middle area. We have no personal offices because I don't believe in them. That was a big one for me. Too often, individuals in established companies seek personal offices as a sign of rank. Everything about our space reflects our collaborative, fast-moving startup culture.

My cube is located right at the center of the office space. It's the same size as everyone else's. There is little on my desk to indicate it is mine. I try to be as mobile as possible, so I can work about anywhere just as easily as I can from the office.

Firing up my laptop, I started the day as I do every day at the office—by looking at my calendar. Scrolling through, I spotted a few "walk-and-talks" with employees (my preferred way to catch up with team members), a client call in the afternoon, and a big blocked-off time slot at 6 p.m. saying, "Matt deciding by end of day!"

My calendar is easily my most important tool. It closely guides how I spend my time, which for a leader is the most precious commodity. My schedule is color-coordinated for various activities. In that way, I can glance at a week and determine if I'm spending enough time in the right places.

The morning was progressing as usual when, around 11 a.m., Martha came up to me. "Morning boss, have you heard about anything going on with RedBrick?"

The reference was to our largest and longest-running client. We practically built our company on being a factor in their incredibly rapid growth.

Martha runs HR for the agency and is one of my most trusted leaders. She was the seventh employee we hired and has been consistently reliable since day one.

"Morning back! No, I haven't. What's up?" I asked.

"Could be nothing, but I got a sense from Steve that the guys at RedBrick might be upset," she said. This news was surprising to me, as Steve had been running the account smoothly ever since we landed it. He is one of those team members who keeps rising to the occasion with each new challenge. Steve is now our top account executive due to how much he has grown RedBrick over the years.

"I'll check with Steve to see what's going on. I'm sure it's nothing, but thanks for the heads-up," I said. Martha is always on high alert and often over-thinks a situation. I wasn't overly concerned.

After texting Steve, "Swing by when you get a moment," I went back to my day.

At about 5:30 p.m., Steve rounded the corner. "What's up boss, saw your text."

Before I could answer, he blurted, "Oh hey, hear from Matt yet? Sure hope we get that one!"

Everybody knew about our pitch to Matt, as well as my follow-up offer to turn Titan around. Most likely half our people thought I was crazy, but they would be eager to hear his answer.

"Nope, not yet. He said the end of the day, so there's still time," I said. He looked at me, nodded, and waited for me to say more.

"Oh, right, I was curious how things are going with RedBrick."

He squinted his eyes and frowned a little. "Why, did you hear something?"

"No, it's just been awhile since you caught me up," I said, telling a half-truth.

He seemed relieved. "Everything is great. The new campaign is off and running, and as you know, we're pitching ideas for the upcoming trade show. The team is pumped about that opportunity. We're meeting early next week to come up with a new round of creative."

"Oh, I thought you guys decided on the trade show approach this past Monday?" I said.

"Yeah, well, you know, sometimes you have to take a few swings at bat before connecting," Steve replied. I could tell there was more to it than that by the way he was having trouble meeting my eyes. "We just need to get the team thinking out of the box a little more."

We were an advertising agency, which meant that we helped our customers market their business to their customers. For a client like RedBrick, we were their Agency of Record, which is the highest commitment an agency can have with a client. For RedBrick, it's an ongoing relationship that spans a wide range of assignments, rather than only specific projects.

"Steve, are you sure?" I started to say, just as the phone began to vibrate on my desk. We both paused and looked over at it. I held up my finger, as if to say hold that thought, and grabbed the phone. It was Matt.

"Hey, Matt," I said. "How's it going?"

"Busy as usual, you know how things are," he said. "You gave me a lot to think about over our coffee yesterday. I got in my car, and my first reaction was, 'this could be really interesting.' By the time I got to work I was thinking, 'this is insane.' Now, after a good night's sleep, I'm… still going back and forth."

43

So far, so good. I had been worried that without me around to deal with his doubts over the last 24 hours he might just drop the idea.

"Yep, I hear you. It's unorthodox, to say the least," I said.

"Are you really sure it's worth five days of my time?" Matt questioned. "I mean, if it's about us hanging out, let's just go to a ball game and have some hot dogs and beer."

"Well, we can do that too," I said. "You know I'm always up for a game. But I truly believe there is nothing more important you can do with your time. If we can pull this off, it could change everything."

"But what exactly does 'pulling it off' mean?" he asked.

I paused for a moment. What ran through my mind was how much Matt had to change at Titan and the conversations with Charles about the essential traits of successful startups. The trick would be to make the transformation happen in such a short time frame.

"We're talking about your fired-up leadership showing the way to energize Titan by changing what's been holding your team back. We can pull it off by meeting just one day a week over the next five weeks. I'll put to use the skills I learned in my years running meetings to solve problems for clients at Ideathon. Think of it as a miraculous Five-Day Turnaround the two of us make happen," I said, perhaps a little more excitedly than I intended.

"You see, Matt," I continued, "the big thing for you, for your company—heck, for most of the traditional corporate world—is that everyone forgets what worked well back when the business first got started. The output becomes stale and jammed with process and, well, boring."

"And the beauty is," I added, "you experienced many of the core traits of successful startups when we worked together at Crackersnap. What we are going to pull off in five days is making that entrepreneurial mindset part of your leadership style again."

The other end of the phone was silent for what seemed like hours.

"And you really think we can get it done?" he asked.

"You bet I do! Come on, tell me you're in, and we'll get down to business."

"Okay! Let's do it!" Matt almost shouted. "Heck, I need something to get me charged up again. If anyone can help me make this happen it's you, with all your career has covered." He paused, then continued. "At the very least, we'll have fun trying."

His voice trailed off as he began clicking on his computer. "Okay, I can commit to an in-person meeting every Monday morning for up to three hours."

"That's perfect," I said.

"Okay, so 8 a.m. to 11 a.m. for five Mondays at my office, and then we'll follow up with a call later in the week. I'll have my assistant create a calendar invite as soon as we hang up. Sound like a plan?" Matt asked.

"You bet it does. Let's lock it in." I learned long ago that when you make the sale, move on as quickly as possible before anyone can reconsider. "See you Monday morning. Looking forward to it."

"Same here, see you then," Matt said, and we both hung up.

The rush of excitement lasted a full minute before I realized how much planning I had to do over the next few days before my first meeting with Matt. I couldn't wait to get started.

DAY ONE

I was 15 minutes out from Matt's office, heading down Hwy 75, and was having trouble containing my anticipation. After I had changed the radio station a few times, I finally shut it off completely and drove in silence.

I had bounced out of bed early, after checking the alarm clock next to my bed seemingly a dozen times throughout the night. I saw 2 a.m., 3 a.m., 3:30 a.m. Finally, my alarm went off at 5 a.m., and I was off like a rocket.

There was so much pressure riding on how this first meeting would turn out. We had to get off to a good start due to the tight timeline.

I pulled into the parking lot of Matt's office, turned off the car, and went over my opening thoughts one more time. At 7:55 a.m., I grabbed my bag and made my way to the front door.

The receptionist was a friendly woman whose smile immediately reminded me of my first-grade teacher, Mrs. Kay. She took my name and handed me a guest badge. She told me Matt wasn't ready for me yet, but she'd let me know when he was.

Sitting in the reception area, I began soaking in the environment. The walls were a beige color with the company logo on the wall behind the receptionist desk. The couch that I was sitting on felt like the kind you'd find in an attorney's office. The oak coffee table had the usual business magazines on it, and there was a large fish tank in the corner.

Drab. That was the word that came to mind. Drab and slightly depressing. Actually, the whole office was like this, I thought, remembering the high-walled cubes and faded carpet.

"He'll be here in just a minute," Mrs. Kay said, breaking me out of my trance.

"Thanks," I said.

A few minutes later Matt bounded around the corner. Like me, he was a morning person.

"You beat me here," I greeted him, shaking his hand.

"Well, I knew you'd get onto me for multitasking during our meeting. So, I got here early to knock out some things," Matt said as he led me down the hallway toward his office.

There was a definite pep in his step this morning. That was a good thing because I was sure this first meeting would be a tough one. From past experience, I knew that once Matt sets his mind on something, it can be hard to get him to change his perspective. Actually, it's one of his strengths—being "all in" on your convictions allows you to act with confidence and speed—but today, he needed to be open to a radical change in his leadership style.

When we got to his office, he asked his assistant, Brian, to hold his calls while we were meeting. I had met Brian many times, and I gave him a quick wave.

We entered, and Matt closed the door behind me.

"All right Matt, ready to get started?" I asked. Despite the energetic and carefree attitude Matt had shown as we made our way back to his office, he didn't seem ready at all.

It was as if he flipped a switch as soon as he sat down at his desk. It wasn't hard to see why. There were a million distractions around him! Two large screen monitors, an Amazon Echo with its blue light circling the top, photos of his family everywhere, stacks of paper and folders in two huge mounds, and Post-it notes on his monitor screens!

I didn't wait for Matt to answer. "Uh, Matt, now that I think about it, let's start with a 'walk-and-talk' session, the way we used to at Crackersnap."

He almost jumped out of his chair. "Great! I know just the path. I take my team on walks there often."

"Terrific." I grabbed my notepad. "Let's both leave our phones in your office, so we don't get distracted."

He grimaced a bit, but accepted my request, and set his phone on his desk as we made our way out of his office.

Strolling back through the hallways of Titan, it was obvious that Matt was a well-liked leader. He casually greeted people, sometimes stopping to introduce me to them. He was always met with a smile. That was a good sign because I was going to ask Matt to do some difficult things, and having a good reputation internally would certainly be required if he was to be successful.

The path was perfect. After a short walk on a makeshift cobblestone walkway, we were presented with a beautiful lake, complete with ducks and several benches.

"It's a half-mile around. I usually do it three or four times with my team members. Gives us a solid 45 minutes to talk out issues," he said.

"Yep, I can see that it's ideal for 'one-on-ones.' Nice and flat— and enough of a commitment when you start a new loop to really get into a good conversation, but not too long that you end up regretting it," I said.

As much as I enjoyed the view, I was eager to get rolling. "Okay, I always find it best to start a meeting by clearly stating the problem that we are hoping to solve. Want to take a stab at that?"

"Sure," Matt said, setting a brisk pace along the path. "Basically, Titan is too big and cumbersome and stuck in its old ways to allow for any significant growth to occur. We're stuck on a hamster wheel of sorts, never really making much progress no matter how hard we run."

I'm a sucker for solid analogies, and Matt had nailed it with that one. I made a mental note to use it myself in the future. But he was wrong about the rest of it.

"Are we really trying to change Titan overall?" I asked, leading the witness.

"Oh, well, I suppose not. We're just talking about my team, aren't we?" he said, nodding his head a bit.

I hesitated to jump in, wanting him to work this one through on his own. Luckily, he continued, "Really the problem we're trying to solve is that my team is too mired in process and bull...sorry, my wife is on me to stop swearing. But we're just way too slow and careful about trying anything new or doing anything that breaks the mold."

I laughed, as I knew his wife and had heard her on more than one occasion get onto Matt for letting a swear word slip out. "Let's tighten what you said a bit. Can you get the problem down to one simple statement?"

He thought for a minute, slowing the pace and kicking a stone into the lake. "In our current state, my team is stuck. We're overly cautious and unable to take advantage of opportunities effectively."

"Yes! Bingo, that's exactly it," I said, truly excited that he had landed on the problem so quickly. "You know Matt, there's an expression I heard recently that nails your situation. It says, 'You can't read the label from inside the jar.' The point is while you're an experienced leader, it's hard 'inside the jar' to step back and get a clear picture of what's holding the team back."

"Can't see the forest through the trees type of thing, I suppose," he said. "That makes sense. Which is why I need you, right Master Yoda?"

I laughed. "Exactly, my young padawan." I couldn't resist a good Star Wars reference.

"So, we know the problem—that your team cannot seriously contribute to growth with its current culture. And the solution I believe will unlock your team's full potential is for them to start acting as if they were working at a startup. As you know, an entrepreneurial mindset is the opposite of how you described the team's outlook. At a successful startup, you move fast, you're not afraid to fail, and you can pivot on a dime."

"Sure, that sounds great. But hey, Will, you surely aren't suggesting that we operate as a startup would? I'm not running my own company the way you are. I can't just walk in this afternoon to start making changes and let the chips fall where they may."

It was a smart point and something that I had wrestled with during countless discussions with Charles. I was ready for the pushback, and I truly believed it was possible.

"Absolutely right. Titan can't operate as a startup, nor would I suggest it do so. If you think about it, startups are working their collective tails off to become the next Titan. What I'm really asking you to do, and I do mean *you*, Matt, is to be much more of an entrepreneur in what you do at Titan. You have to embrace the *Do or Die Mindset* that drives a startup's success. It's the first step in the process we'll be tackling this week."

We were finishing our first lap around the lake, and we cruised right through the turn-off. I took it as a good sign.

"So," Matt said. "You want me to act more like an entrepreneur, even though I don't run my own company."

"Right." I said.

"And you want me to do this how, exactly?"

"I was hoping you'd ask," I smiled. "There are three core steps in gaining a Do or Die Mindset. Want to take a crack at what they might be, or should I just jump right in?"

"Yeah sure, why not," he said. "I'm thinking back to when we worked for Stan at Crackersnap. I always felt he was a first-rate entrepreneur, growing his startup with that fearless confidence you see in great leaders. How about 'fearless confidence'? Is that one of your three parts of the entrepreneurial mindset?"

"Nice! In fact, fearlessness is a core principle, but there's something to address before it. What do you think is necessary to be fearless?"

Matt stopped and scratched his chin, deep in thought. "If you're fearless, I guess that means you're not worried about the consequences? No, that can't be right. Even though Stan was fearless, or at least I perceived him to be so, I think he very much cared about the consequences. I don't know. I think I'm going to need your help with this one."

"Let me tell you a story and see if it helps," I said.

"You and your stories. No wonder you ended up running an advertising agency! Okay, let's hear it," he said, smiling.

For the record, he was right. I do like a good story. I find it helps to emphasize a point and bring the listener deeper into the discussion.

"There was once a small island off the coast of...well, I can't remember where this occurred, but it's a true story...I think. So, there's this island out there, and on this particular beach, it was regarded as a great challenge to see if anyone could swim all the way to it. For years, people would try to make it. The best swimmers would come and start off braving the waves and putting their bodies to the test. One after another would get close to halfway, only to turn around and head back to shore."

"Of course, because at a certain distance you pass the point of no return, and if you give out you just might drown," Matt said.

"Exactly. Then one day this young man comes to the beach to surf, and he hears about the challenge. He looks out at the island and decides to give it a try. He sticks his board into the sand and begins the swim. A crowd begins to form on the beach as he nears the place where others turn around. Only, he keeps going. Eventually, he makes it to the island where he spends the next several hours hanging out. Then he swims all the way back. He's exhausted, for sure, but he makes his way onto the beach to a round of applause and high-fives."

"So, how did he do it?" Matt asks.

"That's precisely what the people on the beach asked him. 'How did you do it when everyone else turned back?' they questioned. 'Why would I turn around?' he asked. 'Because if you didn't make it, you'd surely drown,' someone said. 'Huh, it never occurred to me that I wouldn't make it, so I just kept going,' he said modestly."

I decided to be quiet and let the story sink in for Matt. It didn't take long.

"So, the kid simply believed he would make it. He didn't hedge his bets or look back. He just headed toward the goal with a belief he could make it happen," Matt commented.

"Yep," I said.

"And everyone else had just enough doubt to turn back."

"Yes. They all had a Plan B."

"So, the first trait of a successful entrepreneur is a belief in yourself."

"An Unflinching Belief in Yourself, to be exact," I said.

"Well, I'm a confident person by nature, so I'm not sure this one will be tough for me," he said.

Ah, two steps forward, one step back, I thought.

"Sure, you're a confident leader," I said. "Now think for a minute about what stops you from taking more risks at Titan."

"You mean other than getting fired?" he laughed.

"Well, that's one problem, isn't it?" I said, not laughing back.

"Will, of course I'm worried about being fired. Who isn't?"

"Stan wasn't. And I'm not. Entrepreneurs aren't afraid of getting fired," I replied.

"Of course not, because no one can fire you!" he pointed out.

"Correct, we can't be fired. We can just fail in our business, lose all of our shareholders' money, be forced to let go of our employees, disappoint our families, and carry all the debt that we amassed while launching our business. Yeah, it's much easier to fail as an entrepreneur." I didn't hold back my sarcasm.

"Well sure, but that comes with the job, right? You signed up for that risk as an entrepreneur."

"True. But that doesn't make it any less challenging. And the reason we signed up for that risk is..."

Matt finished my sentence, "...because you have faith in your ability to get the job done."

"Exactly. And, Matt, the chance of an entrepreneur being successful is much lower than you taking a risk and being successful. You know that, right?"

"Of course! They say the chance of a startup succeeding is less than ten percent." He looked at me seriously. "On that note, why exactly do you think acting like a startup—which will almost always fail—is the right path for me?"

"Keep in mind, we're focused on the traits of successful startups, those that make it. These are trends I've analyzed with successful startups that can help leaders like yourself in established businesses move at the speed of a successful startup."

"Yes, I remember. Okay, so the first aspect of the…" he was searching for the right words.

"The *Do or Die Mindset*," I said.

"The *Do or Die Mindset*, thanks. The first aspect is to believe in yourself. An unflinching belief in yourself, as you indicated. I'm on board with that. The second aspect is fearlessness. How is that different from believing in yourself?"

"They're similar but there's an important difference," I said. "Yes, it's true. You can't be fearless without believing in yourself. At the same time, you can believe in yourself and still make decisions based on fear. For example, think of the leader who has unflinching faith in herself but doesn't have confidence in her team. She might be sure of herself and yet she's fearful her team can't deliver. As a result, she makes the conservative, fear-based decision."

I knew this would hit home with Matt, as he's expressed his lack of confidence in his team before.

"Being fearless is easier said than done," Matt commented.

We were completing our third lap at this point, and I was in dire need of a whiteboard to continue the session.

"There's an exercise that can help with being fearless. Let's break off the 'walk-and-talk' here and snag one of your conference rooms. It's time to whiteboard some stuff," I said.

Matt laughed, "So in the first hour you've told one of your classic stories, and now you're going to use a whiteboard. There's only one thing left in the Will trifecta...a latte!"

"Now that you mention it..." I said, grinning.

"Yeah, I'll ask Brian to order us some lattes. I guess I walked right into that one." We headed back toward the Titan building.

After a quick stop in Matt's office to check our messages, we made our way to an available conference room and sat down. A few minutes later Brian brought in our lattes. It was time to get back to day one of The Five-Day Turnaround.

I stood up and made my way to the whiteboard, picking up red and green markers off the ledge. I wrote on top (in green):

Fearlessness

Confidence in being able to handle the worst-case scenario

I turned toward Matt and asked, "What do you think of that definition of 'fearlessness'?"

"Let's see," he said. "So, it's not a belief that the worst-case scenario won't ever happen. Being fearless doesn't mean you're delusional about always getting positive outcomes. You're just confident you can handle whatever comes your way. Right?"

"Right," I agreed. "Someone who is fearless is willing to risk the worst-case scenario because of their belief they can manage it. They have unstinting confidence in their ability to succeed sooner or later."

I then wrote below that:

Worst-case scenarios:

1.

I turned toward Matt and said, "Okay, so if you act more like an entrepreneur—embracing the Do or Die Mindset—what do you perceive to be the worst-case scenarios?"

"Easy, I could lose my job," he said quickly.

I then added to the whiteboard:

Worst-case scenarios:

1. Lose job

"What else?" I asked.

"The company could fail," he said.

I wrote on the board:

Worst-case scenarios:

1. Lose job
2. The company could fail
3.

I looked back at him, waiting for him to give me another suggestion.

After a minute he said, "I might be unhappy or frustrated if I try to act like an entrepreneur and am thwarted at every stop."

"Okay, fair enough," I said, and finished the list:

Worst-case scenarios:

1. **Lose job**
2. **The company could fail**
3. **Poor job satisfaction/unhappiness**

"Now, let me ask you this, Matt. You've progressed at Titan to a position where you have significant responsibility and a decent number of people on your team. Correct?"

"That's right."

"Presumably you've achieved success here based on more than just your winning personality?" I said.

"I am pretty likable most of the time," he joked. "But, yes, I'm confident my superiors would say my progress is based on merit."

"With years of goodwill built up and a solid reputation, do you think that if you start taking some chances and miss once in a while, you'd be fired?" I asked.

He paused to think about that. "You're probably right, as long as my mistakes were not too costly. The more quick wins I get, the more likely I'll be able to take bigger risks later."

I went up to the whiteboard, picked up the green marker and made an addition to number one.

Worst-case scenarios:

1. **Lose job > Unlikely > Focus early on quick wins**
2. **The company could fail**
3. **Poor job satisfaction/unhappiness**

"Let's look at number two: The company could fail." I paused for a second, then I said, "Really? Could the company really fail if you start acting more like an entrepreneur by taking greater marketing risks?"

He paused for a moment and scratched his chin, then said, "No, not really. There's hardly a chance I might do something so disastrous it crippled the company. Just because I'd be operating more like a person running a startup, it's not like I'd suddenly lose my mind just because I picked up some startup traits."

"So, number two isn't something you should be worried about?" I asked, rhetorically.

Worst-case scenarios:

1. **Lose job > Unlikely > Focus early on quick wins**
2. **The company could fail > Highly unlikely**
3. **Poor job satisfaction/unhappiness**

"Well jeez, Will, number three is also kind of a moot point, isn't it? I mean there's poor job satisfaction and unhappiness now! As a reason to be afraid of taking a risk, it seems a bit absurd. I feel silly even having you list it," he said, beating me to the punch.

I chuckled. "Stating our fears is never silly. We're all human. Our emotions help to shape who we are. I've found that sometimes just listing your fears can help you see that they aren't as threatening as they seem."

I went to the board and made the final edit:

Worst-case scenarios:

1. **Lose job > Unlikely > Focus early on quick wins**
2. **The company could fail > Highly unlikely**
3. **Poor job satisfaction/unhappiness > Duh/no change**

Matt grinned at the "duh" part. We could always poke a little fun at each other.

"We've dealt with the first two pieces of the *Do or Die Mindset*—an Unflinching Belief in Yourself and Fearlessness. It's time for the last trait."

I erased the previous exercise on the whiteboard and wrote in big letters:

Results-Oriented

Then I sat down and waited until Matt spoke up.

"'Results-Oriented,' huh? I'm, like, Mr. Results-Oriented. This one should be a piece of cake. I track KPIs and metrics like a hawk, and so does my team. I'm actually relieved, I thought you were on the way to changing me completely!"

He sat back and folded his arms, confident this was going to be easy. As for myself, I was pretty sure he wasn't the type of results-oriented leader he needed to be.

"Yep, you do love a solid metric. I'll give you that."

I needed to ease into this one. "Humor me for a minute. Let's try another exercise."

I walked up to the whiteboard and turned to Matt. "Give me an example of a result you track."

"Easy. Visits to our website from the recent campaign we launched."

I wrote on the whiteboard:

Visits to website

"That's an example of your results-oriented approach, tracking visits to the website, right?"

"Yeah."

"Okay, why do you want visits to the website?" I asked.

"Well, to make more people aware of our products."

Next, I wrote on the whiteboard:

Visits to the website > Product awareness

"And why do you want more product awareness?"

Matt by now felt that the exercise was kind of trite. "Of course it's to get people to buy our products and increase revenue," he said with a raised voice.

"Stay with me. I know this is basic stuff so far, but I'm going somewhere. Trust me," I reassured him.

This time I wrote:

Visits to the website > Product awareness > Customers buy more products

"And..." I started to say, but Matt cut me off.

"And we want customers to buy our products so we can generate more revenue," he said.

I added that to the listing:

Visits to website > Product awareness > Customers buy more products > Increase revenue

"And," he said, not even giving me a chance to start this time, "We want to increase revenue in order to increase Titan's share value."

Another addition to the board:

Visits to website > Product awareness > Customers buy more products > Increase revenue > Increase Titan's share value

"Anything beyond that?" I asked.

"Nope, that's it. Ultimately everything we do in marketing, heck at this entire company, is to increase Titan's share value."

"So then, why isn't that the metric you're tracking?" I asked.

For a moment Matt seemed stunned. "Well, I'm not tasked with doing that, Will. I'm supposed to market what we produce, increasing our brand perception in the market and exceeding revenue goals. Plus, I can't fundamentally affect the share value."

"Wait, you just said that everyone in the company exists to increase shareholder value. You're the Chief Marketing Officer, but you can't affect the share value?" I asked, a bit incredulously.

"That's not what I meant," he fired back. "What I meant is that I can't directly impact shareholder value in a way that I can track. As you know, many forces are impacting the market, and even if I increase revenue for the company, the share value might go down because of some outside factor, like the housing market declining or something."

"Great point. So, in this scenario, increasing revenue would be the highest trackable goal. The key word being 'trackable.'" I erased what was written beforehand and wrote in big bold letters:

Overarching Goal: Increase Trackable Revenue

"Now let me ask you this, when you're considering whether or not to approve an action, do you ask yourself: 'Will this increase revenue for the company?'"

Matt frowned a bit and shook his head. "Honestly, Will, hardly ever. No, wait, I take that back. Never. The only time I even consider that directly is when putting together my annual budget, but even that is surface-level," he said. Matt added, chuckling, "You're not recording this, right?"

"Ha, no, definitely not recording this. Remember, what happens in our meetings stays in our meetings," I said with a grin.

"An entrepreneur," I continued, "is always focused on the big goal. If the efforts they are making are not increasing the big goal, then they stop doing those things and move on to other tactics—"

Matt cut me off. "Because if they don't, their business fails. An entrepreneur has very little room to stay on the wrong path. So, tracking the most important things for their business is critical, right?"

"Exactly! So in that light, what you have to do is keep your team focused on increasing revenue. Use that as a lens every time you're making a decision. Ask yourselves, 'will this action result in increased revenue?' If the answer is 'no,' or 'we aren't sure,' then don't do it."

Matt took in that thought for a bit. "Could be tough, Will. I guess the only way we can see the result is to try it."

"Exactly," I said. "And that's what the rest of this week is for."

The clock on the back wall told me it was almost 11 a.m., the agreed-upon ending time.

I found a blank part of the whiteboard and wrote at the top:

The Do or Die Mindset:

Key traits:

1.

2.

3.

I then turned toward Matt and asked, "Okay, remember what the three traits of the *Do or Die Mindset* are?"

"I think so. The first was a belief in yourself, but you used a particular word to describe that…"

"Unflinching," I said.

"…right, I keep losing that one. The first is *an unflinching belief in yourself*," he said.

I wrote that on the board, then turned back to him.

"The second is *fearlessness*. And the third is *results-oriented*," Matt said.

I wrote it all on the board.

The Do or Die Mindset:

Key traits:

1. Unflinching belief in yourself

2. Fearlessness

3. Results-Oriented

"Excellent work," I said. "Now comes the hard part. You need to start acting on all of this. There are some first steps you can follow to adopt the Do or Die Mindset immediately. In our call on Friday, you can tell me how everything went over the week."

"Bring it on," Matt said. He appeared pleased to have a way to put to use what we accomplished so far on day one. He pulled out his notepad and looked up at me.

"All right, start by spending the rest of today barring any fast-breaking issues you need to tackle, by doing two things. First, spend half an hour listing what you would attempt to do if you were sure you would succeed. That will help you take in the power of believing in yourself."

Matt nodded as he jotted down a note on his pad.

"I also want you to spend time this afternoon reviewing all of the initiatives and campaigns that your team is juggling. Ask yourself, 'Is there anything on this list that we are doing out of fear?' When you find that there are—and you will—I want you to create an action plan to change course immediately. Got it?"

"Roger," he said, making more notes.

"By the end of today, you should have begun reshaping your leadership style and mindset. That will make for a long day one, but I know you can handle it," I said.

"No problem. I want to get the momentum going as soon as possible," he agreed.

"Great. Throughout the rest of this week every single thing that you and your team undertake, I want you to ask, 'Are we doing this because it will increase Titan revenue?' If the answer is 'no,' don't do it. If the answer is 'yes,' get your team to figure out a plan to track the results."

He looked back up at me. "Okay, is that it?"

"That's it for now. Send me a status email tomorrow morning with how things went today. If during the week you feel stuck, send me a note, and we'll work it out."

"Sounds good," he said. We grabbed our stuff and walked back to his office.

I reminded Matt we would be back together again for day two at his office next Monday and he could ping me any time he wanted to reach out before then.

As I walked out of his office, he said, "I doubt I'll have to reach out to you. This should be easy enough. See you next week."

Little did Matt know he'd be calling me, panicked, before the end of the day.

As I drove out of Matt's parking lot and headed back to the agency, I reflected on the morning. Matt had been more receptive than I thought he would be. Perhaps too receptive. I was worried that he thought this would be an easier process than it actually would be. Well, he'd figure that out soon enough. Who knows, maybe it would be easy for him. He did, after all, work at a startup in his previous life.

I pulled into our office parking lot and hopped out of the car. It was approaching 1 p.m., which is when I have my own weekly team leadership meetings. This was my favorite part of the week because it allowed me to make sure all of my team leaders were on the same page and that we were making progress toward our goals.

On entering the office, I immediately felt the buzz of an agency firing on all cylinders. A rapidly growing company has a feel to it that is like nothing else. You can almost sense the electricity in the air.

They were already in the conference room when I arrived. There was Steve, our Head of Client Relationships; Martha, Head of HR; Rachel, Head of Operations; and Ahmet, Head of Business Development. Even though I was a few minutes early—I try never to be late to meetings—they were already in the middle of a heated conversation.

"No, I don't agree with that at all, Steve," said Rachel. "We simply can't afford any more creatives on the RedBrick account. I understand you want to impress them right now, but the entire creative group is spread thin. They're close to a breaking point."

"Creatives are always moaning about how many hours they work," Steve replied. "That's when they do their best work! Besides, I can't imagine they're working on anything more important than RedBrick right now."

"RedBrick is already teetering on the edge of profitability, Steve," she replied. "And it's not exactly…"

"What? It's not exactly what?" he asked.

"Well, it's not exactly the most exciting project these days. Martha, back me up here."

Martha spoke up in her quiet, calming voice. "It's true, many people have expressed that working on the account is stale. They don't feel challenged on it the way they used to. Maybe we should look at rotating people around to give them more creative opportunities?"

"Absolutely not," said Steve. "I'm not moving any of my team on to other accounts. We have too much knowledge built up, and the team works well together. We just need a little more fresh thinking in the mix, that's all."

"Guys," I broke in. "This sounds like the right discussion to have, but let's pause for a minute and do the rundown. Then we can get back into it."

The rundown is how we start each of our leadership meetings. I begin by repeating our core purpose, vision, tenets, and values. Then we go over the latest financial numbers. Each person brings up any issue that needs attention, and we prioritize the issues before diving in.

After completing the rundown—which was fairly tame with no big changes from last week—we identified that RedBrick was the biggest challenge we needed to address.

"Okay, Steve, the floor is yours. Take us through the problem you're trying to solve with RedBrick," I said.

"Well, boss, I wouldn't say there was an exact problem." He sometimes called me boss, usually when he was trying to butter me up. "I was just telling the team here that, if possible, I'd love a little more creative bandwidth on the account. You know how it is, over time you just need some new ideas."

That was true, but I sensed there was more to it.

"Did the client say anything specifically?" I asked.

"No, nothing like that," he said. "I just think we need new ideas."

"Listen, Steve, it would be great if we could free people up to help, but right now I just don't see how we can get it done," said Rachel. She was probably right. Rachel is a detail-oriented operations manager, the best I'd ever hired. If she said we didn't have team members to spare, we probably didn't.

"Besides," she continued, "Ahmet is also asking for creative help for the big new pitch coming up next week."

We all looked at Ahmet, who nodded his head. "You all know how hard it is to win new business. I need our best on this one if we're going to have a chance. Heck, it's tough to win new clients even when we have big creative concepts, like we did with the Titan pitch. Actually, Will, what's the latest with that one?"

Now everyone turned toward me. I began explaining the work I was doing with Matt. It was clear right away that they were shocked by my unusual approach. When I finished talking about The Five-Day Turnaround, Martha raised her hand.

I smiled at her. "Martha, you know you don't have to raise your hand."

"Oh, I know, but you were on such a roll I didn't want to break in," she said. "It's just that our time is up for this meeting, and I need to head out for an interview with a potential new hire."

We gathered up our laptops and notepads and headed for the door. As we walked down the hall, I asked Steve one more time if there was a serious issue with RedBrick. Once again, he said there was nothing wrong. He was just trying to give them a little extra love. I made a mental note to check in with him later in the week.

The rest of the day was fairly uneventful. I used the time to lock down my calendar for the next day and run through my to-do list. I've always found that I'm more successful (and more fulfilled) when I'm aware of what I'm trying to accomplish each day.

I made sure to walk around and interact with the people getting the work done throughout the office. I remembered a rather eye-opening leadership team meeting about six months ago where my team made me aware that I was spending too much time outside the office. I explained that part of my role was networking and business development, requiring me to be out of the office quite a bit. What I had failed to realize was the impact inside the office of my not being present.

Now, it's a part of my daily routine to spend more time in the office and to share what I'm doing out of the office with them.

At 4:30 p.m. my phone started to buzz on my desk. It was Matt.

"Hey, Matt," I said.

"Hey, Will," he said. "Listen, I'm in a big jam and could use your help. Got a few minutes?"

"Of course! What's going on?" I asked. He was talking quickly, and I could sense a bit of panic in his voice.

"Well," he continued, "I did what you said and started listing things that we might be doing out of fear...."

He trailed off, so I asked, "And what did you find? Anything?"

"Oh yeah, for sure," he jumped back in. "There were several things. We were sponsoring some conference out in New Jersey, and I realized we were only doing it because our largest competitor would be there. I went and asked Eric why our competitor was there, and he said he thought it was because one of their clients was attending, and they wanted to make sure we didn't try to poach them."

He laughed. "So they were only attending the conference because we were, and we were only attending because they were!"

"So what did you do?" I asked.

"What do you think? I pulled out immediately. I could tell Eric was a little miffed, but he'll get over it."

So far so good, I thought.

"How did the rest of the day go?" I asked.

"Well, that's just the thing. I was pleased with that decision, but now I've gotten myself into a tough spot.

"We're in the process of rebranding one of our products. When I stopped to think about why, I realized it's because the CEO isn't a fan of the current logo. He said someone at his country club told him it looked like a…" Matt paused for a few seconds, then continued, "The guy said it looks like a dog urinating."

I laughed loudly, not being able to help it.

"He must be pretty… pissed," I said, not being able to resist beating Matt to the pun.

"Yeah, laugh it up, Bucko," he said. "But what am I supposed to do about this?"

"I suppose you have two choices. First, if it does, in fact, remind your customers of a dog urinating, and therefore it hurts the brand and reduces revenue, then you probably do need to change it.

"Second," I continued, "if it does not remind your customers of an over-hydrated Fido, then you're going to have to show your CEO the research, and tell him you don't agree that changing the branding would be useful."

I heard his voice rise at the other end of the phone. "No, of course it doesn't remind them of a dog urinating. We'd never have approved it if any of the focus group research had shown that! And, get this, it's costing us over $125,000 to make all the changes to the current brand!"

"Wow, then I think your next move is pretty clear," I said.

"I know, I know," he said. "I guess I'll try to get on his schedule this week. I knew it was a mistake when he first made the suggestion. I just... didn't have the confidence to tell him so."

I was impressed by his willingness to admit this. Matt is a very confident, and sometimes very proud, guy.

"You know, if it were me, I'd not only make the case to cancel the rebranding project, but I'd also show him what to do with the money we'd save. If you show him why it's a mistake and how you can make additional revenue for Titan with the savings, I bet he'd go for it," I said.

"Great idea," Matt said. "I actually have a few projects I want to kick off that could bring in new revenue. Okay, I'll go for it and keep you posted about how it turns out."

"Terrific, talk to you soon," I said, and hung up.

I sat back in my chair and reflected on the give-and-take in the phone call. Matt was taking this seriously. His willingness to confront the CEO was huge. Maybe there was hope for this to work out after all.

At the office Tuesday morning, there was an alert signaling an email in my inbox from Matt. The subject was *Day One Progress*.

It had slipped my mind that I asked him to send me an update letting me know how his first day had gone. Excitedly, I opened the email. It read:

Will,

Enjoyed yesterday morning immensely, and I'm glad we're on this journey.

Overall, it was an enlightening experience from start to finish. Laying out what I would do differently, if I were sure I would succeed, was interesting. And reviewing what the team's doing for Titan out of fear allowed me to cancel several flawed initiatives.

Lastly, let me know if 3 p.m. on Friday works for us to touch base at the end of the week. I'll share more of what's happening then.

Thanks,
Matt

My preference for email was to be quick and to the point to save both parties time, so I wrote back:

Excellent progress, and thanks for sharing.
Yes, 3 p.m. works for Friday, talk then.

Best,
Will

Almost immediately after Matt had agreed to join in our attempt at pulling off The Five-Day Turnaround, I sent a text to my mentor Charles asking if he was available to get together. His input could be invaluable in making this happen.

His response was, "Sure, I can meet for lunch at Naan Place at noon on Friday. See you then."

"Great, see you then!" I replied.

Charles and I first met when serving on a small committee of technology and marketing leaders. The group was created to spur economic growth in our town. Unfortunately, the meetings were poorly run, and the committee disbanded after a handful of sessions. The positive takeaway was my admiration for how Charles handled himself in those meetings.

There was a moment in our second meeting when I first really took notice of Charles. There had been a debate about the progress made so far—and there were several ideas on the table going back and forth.

I was starting to lose interest, as it seemed like we were talking in circles and getting nowhere. Then Charles stood up and walked to the whiteboard, which had been blank until this point. Everyone kind of got silent as he quietly picked up a marker and wrote on the whiteboard:

What Gets Measured, Gets Done

He sat down and said, "In all my years in business, one thing always remains the same: What gets measured, gets done. It seems that in the past nothing was ever put in place to measure results, and, therefore, we have no idea if we've been successful in our efforts. We've been talking for hours about what we could do in the future, but we haven't laid out what the success metrics should be. Until we do that, it doesn't matter what we do, because it won't be successful."

I loved his reasoning, but my colleagues seemed to miss the point entirely. They commented, "Good stuff, Charles," then went back to debating the benefits of various plans of action. There was nothing further said about how to measure results.

I made it a point to connect with Charles after the meeting, and he was happy to get together. I essentially adopted him as my mentor. We got together every few months for coffee or lunch. I would pick his brain on any number of things that I was facing. He was always gracious and thoughtful, and he helped me find my way over many rough spots in the years we've known each other.

Along the way, we started to look at the difference between my corporate clients and my startup clients. The startup clients were always moving fast to gain an advantage, with a willingness to disrupt their own business in the spirit of open-ended progress. On the flipside, my corporate clients were always complaining about their inability to move at anything more than a slug's pace, their propensity to be stalled by a fear of change, and their insane number of meetings.

Before long, we started dialing in on the core traits we felt were required for established firms to move at the speed of a startup. The list had started at 12, then came down to seven, and recently we simplified them to five core traits.

I was excited to share with Charles my proposal to Matt, and I wasn't sure if he would think I was a genius or out of my mind. Or maybe a little of both.

○⌒○

I woke up Friday morning thinking about what I would say to Charles. At the office, I was able to clear my inbox and make some changes to the agency's evolving website. On the way out, I swung by Steve's desk to pick back up the conversation about RedBrick, but he wasn't there.

At 11:45 a.m., I pulled into the parking lot of Naan Place. I arrived early because I never want to keep anyone, especially Charles, waiting.

Naan Place was a fairly unassuming Indian restaurant, and I found myself having lunch there a few times a month. It was quiet, the food was good, and it was close to my office. I was a creature of habit in many ways.

A few minutes later Charles strolled into the restaurant, and I saw him scan the room looking for me. He was tall, probably 6'2" or 6'3," with a head full of brown hair just beginning to turn grey. He was in great shape, always cycling and running, making it hard for me to pin down his age. My guess would be early sixties. If someone told me he was in his midforties, I would only be surprised because of how much he has accomplished creating new ventures.

Charles caught my eye, waved, and made his way over to my table.

"Will, great to see you," he said, shaking my hand vigorously. "It's been, what, over a month? I was beginning to wonder if you had forgotten about your old friend."

"Ha, not at all! I just thought you might need time to recover from your cycling trip in South Africa. What was that—like 250 miles in total?" I asked.

"240, actually. We did 60 miles a day for four days. It was incredible, the most spectacular views in the entire world. I can't wait to go back," he said.

"I bet. Sounds amazing. Maybe after I've sold a few more businesses like you, I'll start taking some trips like that," I said as he sat down.

He unrolled his napkin and placed it on his lap, took a sip of his water, leaned into the table toward me and said, "Will, life is a string of experiences, and we're here to enjoy them. Never get so caught up in work that you forget how much more there is to explore. I so wish I had taken time while I was building my companies to travel the world and have these kinds of experiences as a younger man. It's so much healthier than simply focusing on business success," he said, putting air quotes around "business success."

"I hear you. You're right. But you know how it is, I love building my business right now. It's really both my job and my hobby! Making sure that I spend enough quality time with Sarah and Danielle fills up the rest of my time. But you're right; we'll try to make sure we find time to experience the world before we get much older. Of course, if I have your energy at your age, we'll be able to travel all we want!" I said.

"How is Danni doing?" he asked. He had called my daughter that since she was born four years earlier. "And how's Sarah doing?"

"They're both great. Danielle is playing junior soccer, which is a riot. Sarah is coaching, which is equally fun. Watching her chase six four-year-olds around a soccer field for an hour is entertaining, to say the least. They're both out of town for another week visiting my in-laws," I said.

The server came up and asked us what we'd like to eat. After we ordered, I jumped into it, explaining what had transpired with Matt up to this point. Listening to myself talk, I realized how crazy it all sounded. Could this really be done in just five days of meetings?

Our meal came, and, as we began to eat, Charles said, "So, it was our conversations over the past months that led you to believe you can bring about the turnaround so quickly, huh?"

"Oh, I'm sure that played a role, though I think I was also just desperate to get the win with Matt.

"Do you think it can be done?" I asked nervously.

"I definitely believe it can happen. Doing it with only five meetings is what's tough. But what's life for if not tackling next-to-impossible situations!" he said, with a grin that looked a bit mischievous. I could tell he was fired up about the challenge.

"Okay," he continued, "so, you met with Matt on Monday, and you get four more meetings with him. Well, that's perfect since we are getting close to identifying the five core startup traits for him to master."

"Right, so the best plan would seem to be tackling each of those traits one day at a time in the way the first Monday went. Then we'll see if Matt can make significant progress between the meetings," I noted.

"But," I continued, "we have only really nailed the first trait, the Do or Die Mindset. I feel good about that one based on how receptive Matt was to it, but the rest are all in various stages of completion. Do you think over the next month you can be available for lending some support? It's likely I'm going to get stuck a few times."

"Of course. My time is limited as I have a number of strong commitments. But I can carve out time to get together maybe once a week or so," he said.

"That's terrific," I responded. "Thanks so much."

We looked at our calendars and blocked out dates over the next month.

"Just one thing more," I broke in. "For the second meeting with Matt, I'm planning to use the PVTV trait you introduced to me. It's worked like a charm in getting everyone on the same page at my shop. Do you think that's a good choice for Day Two?"

"Absolutely! Everything else hinges on getting that one right," was his quick response. "You've already seen what arriving at a clear take on Purpose, Vision, Tenets, and Values has done for your success at the agency."

After we made some more small talk, the server took our plates and dropped off the check.

Charles grabbed it off the table. He always paid, no matter how much I protested. As we stepped outside onto the curb, he said, "You know, Will, this is going to be a great experiment. In all the years I've been in business, there's never been a challenge quite like it! I'll see you next week, and good luck on Monday with PVTV."

I'm sure his comments were meant to get me excited, but the idea that Charles had never seen anything like this before was unsettling for a moment. But only for a moment because I loved a challenge.

It was time to get to work.

Friday at an advertising agency is always high energy. Given that we placed a high emphasis on work-life balance at my firm, everyone worked extremely hard on Fridays to give themselves the best chance of not having to work over the weekend.

The phone rang right on schedule—Matt and I had agreed to talk at 3 p.m. I answered quickly.

"What's up, Matt?" I said, trying to conceal my excitement (and nerves) to hear how the week had progressed.

He laughed briefly. "Oh, you know, nothing much. Just changing how I do everything, apparently."

"Oh yeah, about that," I said. "Tell me how it went!"

"Overall, I have to admit it was rather refreshing. I'd say, even though there were a few rough spots which I'll share with you in a minute, it was probably one of the most gratifying weeks I've had in a long time. Even my wife commented on my chipper demeanor yesterday," he said.

"That's just great, Matt," I said, knowing that for this process to work, the leader would have to feel engaged and motivated.

"So, what was the biggest challenge this week?" I asked.

"On Monday when I called you, I would have said it would be the conversation with the CEO around the new branding project. But that actually went far better than I expected," he said.

"Did he go for shelving the project?"

"Not right away. We debated back and forth about the merits of the project. I could see it was going nowhere after about 30 minutes. So, I went to the whiteboard and asked him, 'Tell me, Bruce, how much revenue will the company make if we go through with the rebranding?' I wrote on the whiteboard: 'Revenue Produced,' and drew a line under it. Then, next to it the words: 'Cost of Project,' and under that '$35,000 + $90,000 = $125,000.'"

"What do those two numbers represent?" I asked.

"That's exactly what he asked," Matt said. "The first number is what we have spent so far, and the second number is what we will spend to finish the rebranding."

"Ah, excellent," I said. "What happened next?"

"Well, of course, he had no answer for how much revenue we would expect from the rebranding project. Then he fell right into my trap when he asked me—for the first time—what I thought. My response was to write '$0' on the whiteboard under 'Revenue Produced,'" Matt proudly said. I swear, I could hear him smiling through the phone.

He continued, "Bruce asked me why I never said anything before. At first, I told him it was because nobody asked. Then I corrected myself and said I didn't feel confident enough to speak up.

"Sensing he was moving in my direction, I decided to hit him with the Sunk Cost Fallacy. As you know, it says just because you have invested money in something does not mean you should continue with it only for that reason. After a while, if an investment doesn't seem right, how much you've spent on it doesn't matter. You should shut it down."

I was well aware of the Sunk Cost Fallacy. In fact, I probably was the one who told Matt about it. But seeing it put to use was different from just talking about the concept. This was getting interesting.

Then Matt paused and said something I'll never forget. "Bruce hit me with, 'So, you're saying that because you weren't confident enough to speak up when I was pushing this project, it cost me $35,000?'"

"Whoa," I said, knowing full well his CEO was right in asking that question. "How did you respond?"

"I sucked it up and agreed with him. He came back with, 'Well, never let it happen again. From now on, you tell me how you truly feel about something, and I promise to hear you out. Now, what are you going to do with the $90,000 you just saved me?' After walking him through the projects I was proposing, each with a corresponding expected revenue goal—something he'd never seen from me before—he greenlit the projects on the spot!"

"That's great!" I commented. "It's funny to say this, but I'm proud of you man!"

"All right, all right, don't get all kumbaya on me now," he said. "I could use your help with something else though."

"What's that?" I asked.

"Well, as we discussed, everything my team was doing throughout the week was put through the two questions, 'Are we doing this out of fear?' and 'Is this going to drive revenue for the company?' Throughout the process, one of my team leads, Eric, kept pushing back at me."

I had met Eric before and knew him to be very smart. Yet I could see him being rigid and likely to want to stick with the usual way of getting things done.

"How did you respond when he pushed back?" I asked.

"Well, I kept insisting he show me how the projects would drive revenue, which is sometimes a hard thing to do when you're talking about marketing. He'd then counter by asking if I believed in the power of a brand, which of course I do. I mean, eventually, I would win the argument because I'm his boss, but I would sure like him to be on board."

"What about Meredith, how did she react?" I was asking about Meredith because I knew she was his other direct report, and she had made copious notes during our pitch to Matt.

"Oh, she loved the idea. Absolutely loved it. She was 'all in' from the moment I explained the process. I think her excitement is part of what made Eric push back a bit," he said.

"I tell you what, for Monday's meeting, bring Eric and Meredith to the session as well. It will give me a chance to see both of their reactions in person and try to course-correct them if need be," I said.

"Good idea, I'll do that," Matt said. "Otherwise, it was a great week, and I can't wait to see what you have in store for me on Monday."

"Me, too," I joked. I had a whole lot of prep to do over the weekend to prepare for our second meeting.

"I'll see you bright and early Monday morning," I said.

"You got it," he said and hung up.

I sat back in my chair, relieved. Matt's excitement over the process was surprising.

It would be hard to get into anything else after our conversation, so I decided to head home to go for a jog, clear my head, and start thinking about Day Two.

DAY TWO

Once again, I was eager to get to Matt's office. Throughout the weekend if I wasn't preparing for today's meeting, I was thinking about it in the back of my mind.

I wanted to be sure last week's momentum was not lost. It was surprising how quickly Matt had embraced the concept of the Do or Die Mindset. I had feared that Corporate America had changed Matt for the worse—maybe permanently.

On the drive, I ran over my plan for the day. Having Meredith and Eric join in would be a benefit, but it also was a cause for concern. We urgently needed his team to be invested in making The Five-Day Turnaround a success. What if they chose to resist the process?

Once again, I made it to Matt's office early—and, once again, Mrs. Kay (she would forever be Mrs. Kay in my mind) happily greeted me in the lobby. She informed me that Matt was already there and would see me shortly.

As I waited in the lobby, Meredith arrived. I wasn't in her direct line of sight, so she wasn't aware of my presence. She seemed in a good mood, ready to make the most of our time together that day. I began to wonder if Eric was at the office when I saw him emerge from the entryway. He almost immediately took notice of me as well.

"Hi Will," he said, as he made his way over to me. "I'm excited about our meeting today."

We shook hands, and I gave him a friendly smile. "It's great to have you and Meredith as part of the process," I said.

"Let me take you back to the conference room," he offered, leading me out of the lobby. "I believe we have coffee and bagels ordered."

I was a bit surprised by how pleasant he seemed. Not that I expected him to be rude, but I expected some initial resistance. So far, so good, I thought.

Eric dropped me off in the conference room and went to check into his office. I had a few minutes to set things up before the meeting would start. Today would be critical. It would set the foundation—quite literally—for how Matt's team would unlock their ability to act like a successful startup within the confines of a mature corporation.

Matt came into the room first. We exchanged hellos as he plopped down in one of the chairs at the conference table. "Any initial tips regarding Eric and Meredith before we get started?" I asked.

"Well, they're both really sharp, but very different. Eric has a great deal of experience, runs branding and advertising for me. He's been here since I arrived...what, five years ago? Meredith, as you know, is my newest resource hire, and she leads the PR and communications team."

I made a mental note to talk to Matt about the use of the word "resource," and then asked, "How did they react when you briefed them on the process and our meeting today?"

Matt smiled and said, "Meredith was very pleased. She's a sponge for new ideas. Eric was... somewhat skeptical. But that's to be expected. He's like that with anything new."

Just then, both Meredith and Eric entered the room. We greeted each other and, after everyone got settled, it was time to kick off the meeting.

"Meredith and Eric, thank you for joining us this morning," I said. "I'd like to start by asking you both this question—why do you think we're here?"

Eric jumped in first. "You're trying to help us figure out how we can...how did you put it, Matt? Think differently so we can work with your agency on the campaign."

Matt started to comment, but I signaled to let their response continue without his input. "Is that what you think, Meredith?" I asked.

"Kind of, yes. My take is that you're going to lead us through some brainstorming exercises to help Eric and me be more creative in tackling the new project," she said.

"You're both on the right track, but not quite on target," I responded. "This discussion is much bigger than me trying to unlock your creative ability to run the campaign that my agency pitched."

There were two whiteboards in the room; one large one in the center and a second smaller one on the side wall. I went to the large whiteboard and at the top in all caps wrote:

THE GOAL: TO ACT MORE LIKE A SUCCESSFUL STARTUP

I underlined "successful" and turned back to them to ask, "Why do you think that Matt and I believe Titan should try to act more like a smart, successful startup?"

"Because we don't innovate enough anymore?" Meredith offered.

Before I could comment, Eric said, "We innovate all the time. Just last quarter we rolled out a new digitized package design. We were the first in our industry to deploy that kind of thinking. Last year we were recognized as one of the most innovative companies by the largest trade publication in our sector."

"For sure. You are known in the industry as an innovator, there's no doubt," I said. "But a successful startup does more than innovate. In fact, a startup's success has very little to do with innovation and much more to do with how quickly they pivot to create and adopt change. They're nimble, focused, and unified in what they're trying to achieve. Are those things you can say about Titan overall? Or about your team in particular?"

Matt laughed. "No, I don't think any of us would use those words to describe either Titan or our team. Do you guys agree?"

Both Meredith and Eric nodded their heads.

I needed to make sure they were really on board for getting this done before I moved forward. "Does that make sense to you two? Matt and I believe your team can focus on the most critical areas and move fast in helping Titan grow as if you were a successful startup. Any disagreements with that?"

Again, they nodded in agreement, with Meredith taking notes along the way.

"Great. So, the first thing we need to do is create alignment within the team, which is today's mission. Every successful startup has a construct that clearly states why the company is in business, what type of company it wants to become and how it's going to achieve that goal. Most important are the values that guide the team along the way," I said.

I wrote on the board,

- **Purpose**
- **Vision**
- **Tenets**
- **Values**

I then added a descriptor to each word:

- **Purpose—Why we exist**
- **Vision—What we want to become**
- **Tenets—How we're going to do it**
- **Values—Guide us along the way**

"How are Purpose and Vision different?" Meredith asked.

"Great question," I said. "You can think of it like this: a company's Purpose is the change it wants to create in the world, and the Vision is the company it needs to become to bring about that change. During the pitch process, I was pleased to discover that Titan has a very tight and compelling Purpose and Vision. Most large corporations have long, obtuse ways of describing their business." I paused. "Do either of you know what Titan's Purpose and Vision are?"

Neither of them spoke up. Meredith shook her head "no." I wasn't surprised. "Okay. Here's the problem," I said. "Even if you have a nice way of talking about your company, if you don't operationalize it, there's no reason to have it."

I walked over to the smaller whiteboard and wrote:

Titan

- **Purpose: To bring families closer together**
- **Vision: To be the leading global CPG brand**

"Here's how it works," I explained. "Titan exists to bring families closer together. How are they going to do that? By becoming the leading global CPG brand. As Titan gets closer and closer to becoming 'THE'—notice I didn't write 'A'—leading global CPG brand, they'll be more successful in bringing families closer together."

"Okay. I didn't know the exact wording, but I do know the gist," Matt said. "I've heard our CEO, Bruce, talk about this a few times, usually when he wants to push a decision one way or the other. If you think about our products, they all do point toward bringing families closer together. Some more directly than others."

"Right," I said. "What I couldn't find, though, is a set of tenets or strategic pillars that clearly state how you're going to achieve the Vision. Does something like that exist, Matt?"

"Not that I know of, which I suppose is a huge problem! Either they exist, and somehow I'm not aware, or they don't exist," he said.

"Yep, spot on," I said. "I did find a statement of Titan's Values. They're basically a carbon copy of what almost every large corporation says. That's not really a problem, provided they are being brought to life on a daily basis."

I wrote on the whiteboard:

Values:

- **Honesty**
- **Forward-thinking**
- **Dependability**
- **Commitment**

"I've certainly seen those before," said Meredith. "I think they're part of a poster on the wall outside my office. I wouldn't say there's been much talk about values, though."

Now Eric weighed in. "But do values really matter? I mean, in the end, isn't it all just 'be a dependable person and work hard'?"

"Let's put a pin in that, Eric," I said. "When they're done right, Values are quite powerful and necessary. The problem is, they are often only there because it's a business practice to have defined Values. But let's go back to Purpose and Vision."

I walked back over to the big whiteboard. "We are here to help you—the marketing team at Titan—think and act more like a successful startup. To do that, your team needs a unifying platform. It has to be in alignment with, but not the same as, the company's defined approach."

"We do that by keeping the company's Purpose in mind," I continued, "And creating your own team Vision."

I wrote:

Titan marketing team:

- **Purpose: to bring families closer together**
- **Vision: _____**

"Let's start with this. Eric, why don't you come up to the small whiteboard and lead the team in an exercise," I said, eager to get Eric actively involved. He'd been silent for a while, and I could tell his interest was lagging. (It was clear that I would have to make full use of the skills I had developed in my years at Ideathon running group problem-solving meetings.)

He walked up and grabbed a marker, and I got him started. "Okay, begin by listing the things your team needs to do to help Titan 'bring families closer together.'"

"We have to build a product-market fit," Matt said.

"Great. So, Matt, can you break that down for us a bit?"

"Sure, it means we have to be certain that the products we launch are going to be something that our customers honestly need in their lives and will spend money on."

Eric wrote "Product-market fit" on the board.

"Great, what else?" I asked.

"Have solid ROI," said Eric, writing that on the board. "We have to make sure that we are spending the company's money wisely."

"Excellent," I said.

"Support the product teams?" Meredith pitched in.

"Oh yeah, good point," Matt responded. "We definitely have to work well with the internal teams at Titan if we want to make things happen. Understanding their needs and how we can help them is a big one."

Eric wrote "Support product teams" on the board.

"Ok, any other big buckets we might be missing?" I asked.

No one could think of anything else, so I said, "Okay, your team must determine how the products you market improve the lives of your customers. You must run an ROI-positive department. And you need to be good partners with internal teams. I like how you came up with the core Tenets to achieve your team's Vision! Eric, can I have the marker please?"

He handed me the marker and took his seat. I went to the large whiteboard and wrote:

Titan Marketing Team:

- **Purpose: To bring families closer together**
- **Vision:** _____

Tenets:

- **Find product-market fit**
- **Focus on ROI**
- **Maintain healthy internal partnerships**

"The Tenets in your PVTV are the core activities that will allow us to achieve our Vision. It's okay that we ended up identifying our Tenets before getting to Vision. What do we think about these Tenet activities?" I asked.

Meredith responded, "Actually, we have to maintain more than just good internal partnerships, we have numerous external partners as well. Can we remove 'internal' from that last one?"

I looked to Matt, and he gave me the nod, so I erased "internal."

"Eric, anything we're missing?" I asked.

He looked intently at the board and said, "I suppose we could consider something around generating awareness. I'm thinking of the things we do, like branding initiatives, creating campaigns, press releases...I'm not sure that 'generate awareness' is covered by the other three tenets." He paused for a minute and continued with confidence, "Yeah, we need a fourth Tenet."

I agreed and glanced over to Matt to gauge his response. He was nodding. I was pleased that he seemed invested and had done so well.

"Definitely. We should add that one to the list," Matt said.

I went back to the whiteboard:

Titan Marketing Team:

- **Purpose: To bring families closer together**
- **Vision: _____**

Tenets:

- **Find product market fit**
- **Focus on ROI**
- **Maintain healthy partnerships**
- **Generate product awareness**

Once everyone had agreed, I said, "Okay, excellent work everyone. Let's take a short break and come back in 15 minutes."

The three of them left the room, and I had a few minutes to reflect on the progress thus far.

Several years back, I picked up the tip of taking a meeting break from another CEO. We were talking about how to be more effective in meetings. He shared this nugget of advice with me: "Whenever I'm leading a meeting that runs more than a few hours, I schedule a break at least halfway through. The time allows people to do things like check email and use the restroom. Mostly, though, it allows me to regroup. It's especially important when I'm participating in the meeting as well as leading it. It helps me avoid getting caught up in the conversation and veering off track without realizing it. Taking a break allows me to assess where we are so I can stay on track."

I always remembered that advice. Reflecting on our progress so far, I thought we were doing pretty well. And I was pleasantly surprised with how little pushback I was getting from Eric.

That optimistic view didn't last long.

Matt and Meredith came into the room just shy of the 15-minute break time. Eric came in several minutes past the time allotment. My reaction was not to make a big deal of it, as I didn't want to get back into the process on the wrong foot.

"Okay, let's take a look at where we are," I said. "We have four key Tenets that will help the marketing department at Titan reach our goals. But, we haven't nailed down what the overall objective is for our team. That's the Vision in PVTV."

I walked up to the whiteboard and asked the team, "Looking at our Tenets—finding product-market fit, generating awareness in the marketplace, striving for positive ROI, and maintaining healthy relationships…why are we focusing on those particular initiatives?"

Eric rolled his eyes, sighed audibly, and glanced down at his phone on the table. I was about to call him out for it when Meredith chimed in with a guess.

"Is it to market the company better?" she asked.

"And why do we want to market the company better? Let's take it up a notch," I said.

"I'll jump in," Matt said. "Will and I went round and round on this last week. Ultimately, I thought it would be to increase shareholder value, but that was too abstract. At the end of the day, our job is to grow revenue for the company."

"I'm sorry, but in my experience, that's not something that marketing should be accountable for," Eric said.

"Why do you think that, Eric?" I asked.

"Because that's the job of the sales team," he continued. "That's why they're the sales team, and we're the marketing team. We can do an amazing job, but if the sales team doesn't pick the ball up and run with it, then we can't do anything to bring in revenue."

Now we were getting somewhere.

"Okay, that's a valid point. Let me ask you this, how do you know if you did a terrific job?"

Eric had an annoyed look on his face as he fired back, "If our advertising tests well, if our communications get a high number of downloads, and if the industry acknowledges our work through awards, all of those things mean we did a great job."

"Got it," I said, writing those things down on my notepad. "I think we can all agree that those are good indicators that our marketing efforts are on the right track—"

Eric cut me off. "Not on the right track, they are the right track. If we win an ADDY, we know we did impressive work."

ADDYs are one of the top marketing awards you can win. More than 40,000 submissions come in every year. My agency had been runner-up a few times.

"So then you'd maintain that the goal of marketing at a company is to…" I paused for a second, then continued, "…win marketing awards. Is that right?"

A second eye roll. "No, of course not," he said.

"But you just told me that you know you're doing a great job if you win an ADDY for the work. So that must be the goal then, right?" I was trapping the witness, but it had to be done.

He was visibly frustrated now. "You know that's not the goal. The goal is to market our brand, so we sell more products. Fine, but I still don't see how we can do the sales team's job for them."

"We'll get to that part, but first let's finish nailing down our Vision statement. Meredith, do you want to take a stab at what the Vision might be?" I asked.

"Sure," she said. "How about: Our Vision is to increase sales of more products for the company."

"Technically, it doesn't have to be more products. We could sell higher-priced products but sell fewer of them," Matt broke in.

"Oh, so then maybe it's: Our Vision is to generate revenue for the company," Meredith said. "Wait, what about this. Our Vision is to consistently generate revenue for the company? Matt is always talking about consistency across everything we do."

"Love it," Matt said, with a smile.

"Thanks!" I said, writing her statement on the board.

Titan Marketing Team:

- **Purpose: To bring families closer together**
- **Vision: To consistently generate revenue for the company**

Tenets:

- **Find product market fit**
- **Focus on ROI**
- **Maintain healthy partnerships**
- **Generate product awareness**

"So, here is how you might sum it up," I said. "Let's see how it sounds and if we're missing anything."

"Our Vision is to consistently generate revenue for the company. We will do this by finding product-market fit, generating product awareness, focusing on ROI, and maintaining healthy relationships. Thoughts?"

Eric argued, "We could do all of that, and the sales team could be inept. I still don't see how we can really impact revenue with them in the way."

"First things first," I said. "We need to start thinking of the sales team as our partner, not a group that's 'in the way' or 'inept.' Second, I do think you have a point. Our last Tenet is to focus on healthy relationships, but I don't think that's specific enough. You have a real partner in sales that must be able to take advantage of the tools that your team gives them."

I stopped there and waited for someone to jump in. It took a few minutes, but Matt finally said, "How about something like, 'Empower our sales team toward success'?"

I let that hang in the air for a minute, then looking at Eric and Meredith said, "What do you guys think?"

"What do you mean by 'empower,' Matt?" Meredith asked.

"We have to educate and train them to use our tools. We also need to get feedback from them about what we can do to help them do better. They might tell us things we never thought of before to help them be more successful," he said.

"Have you ever done this with the sales team?" I asked, genuinely curious.

"I'm embarrassed to say we have not! That's crazy, now that I think of it," Matt said.

"But they should be coming to us and suggesting what's needed, right? Our job isn't to help them do their job!" Eric said, obviously exasperated by this line of discussion.

"Well, that's certainly one way to think of it. In my experience, that's the typical way that someone in a large, established company would assess the situation," I said. "Instead of everyone being in it together and working toward a common goal, people fall into the pattern of thinking that their job is to have individual or at best team success, but not overall company success.

"In a successful startup," I continued, "this kind of thinking does not, or at least cannot, exist. If people are thinking solely about themselves or their team, and not making sure they are helping the company hit its goals, then the startup will fail. Everyone needs to be doing everything they can to help the company succeed."

"I've been a victim of this type of thinking. Back at my past company," Matt said, addressing Eric directly, "we were all in it together. While I was running marketing, I sometimes did customer service calls because that's what was needed at the time. And you know what? It was invigorating. We moved fast and solved problems, and it felt like we were all winning together. At Titan, we don't have that mentality. Now I see that my attitude and mindset have slipped into this 'corporate' way of thinking."

He sat back, and everyone was silent for a minute. I was really proud of Matt for admitting that to his own team.

It was time to wrap up the day's session.

"Matt, thank you for sharing. I want to help your team unlock your ability to think and act like entrepreneurs. At this point, some of you may be more skeptical than others," I said, turning to Eric. Everyone laughed, diffusing whatever tension was left. "I'm sure we can get there. We just have to be committed to the process and supportive of each other along the way."

With that, I finished writing what was on the board:

Titan Marketing Team:

- **Purpose: To bring families closer together**
- **Vision: To consistently generate revenue for the company**

Tenets:

- **Empower our sales team toward success**
- **Find product market fit**
- **Focus on ROI**
- **Maintain healthy partnerships**
- **Generate product awareness**

"I moved the sales team action to the top Tenet. If you don't get that one right, you won't be successful overall.

"We're getting close to time here, and I appreciate all the effort you've put in this morning. As a group, you have a few homework assignments," I continued.

"The next thing you have to do is create your team Values. Model them after the company's Values, but make them your own. Think about the qualities and characteristics you'll need to achieve your Vision and Tenets, and what values you want your team members to exhibit. Do this effort with the entire marketing department, not just the three of you. From that point, you need to start bringing your PVTV to life."

I turned to Matt. "If you have a few minutes after we finish up, I'll share some ideas about how to make these things happen."

Eric said, "I don't mean to sound negative, but we have a big deadline on Friday, and this sounds like something that can wait. How about we push this back until next week?"

Thankfully, before I could answer, Matt spoke up. "No, this is critical. We will figure out how to make time for it. There are probably other things we can de-prioritize, but this is not one of them. We're fully committed as a team to executing against this."

"Great. Thanks again for the time, everyone. I promise this effort will be worthwhile." Eric and Meredith started packing up their stuff, while Matt and I waited for them to leave the room.

"Hey man, look, sorry about Eric's attitude today. I'll talk to him about it," Matt said.

"Seriously, it's okay. I expected pushback on doing this with such a tight deadline. As long as he participates, it's healthy to have a skeptic in the group to keep us honest. He made some good points," I said.

"Well, I appreciate that, but I'll still talk with him," he said. "I gotta say, this was a productive morning. I was unaware of how our relationship—or lack of relationship—with sales was impacting our performance. The first thing I'm going to do is reach out to Ann and talk about how to bring our two departments closer together." Ann was their Head of Sales.

"That makes sense," I agreed. "Let's take a minute to talk about how to operationalize your team's PVTV." Matt agreed, so I continued.

"Once you've nailed the Values part, you'll need to come up with some ways to share what the three of you accomplished here today with your full team. It could be through the notecards you pass out or posters—whatever makes the most sense for you. Understand?"

"Yep, we're a creative group, I'm sure we can come up with a few cool ways to do that," he said.

"Next, and this will feel awkward at first, but I promise it gets easier each time, is to start each meeting you have by reciting the PVTV. It doesn't matter if it's with a few members or the entire team. This is the first thing you do. Ultimately, it would be best if you memorized the guideline word for word. You want to deliver it without notes while looking people in the eyes."

"I haven't memorized anything word for word since the Pledge of Allegiance, but okay," he said with a laugh.

"If you feel the need to stand up with your hand on your heart when you deliver the PVTV, then go for it," I said, laughing as well.

"The final thing you'll need to do is use your five Tenets as the agenda for your overall team meetings. You should use that lens as a way to talk about how your team is doing and your core focus. Make sense?" I asked.

Matt nodded. "I think I can do all of that," he said, making notes in his notepad.

"So how about you send me an email tomorrow morning with a recap of how the rest of the day plays out. I'll get back to you with a few points about ways to run your team meeting to nail down the Values in the PVTV. You can update me once you are finished. Let's talk by phone again Friday afternoon so you can share how the week went. If you get stuck along the way, feel free to ping me," I said.

"Perfect," Matt concluded, standing up and getting his things together. "You ready to go?"

"Not yet, I want to make a few notes while the meeting is still fresh in my mind," I said.

Matt left, and I stayed behind to reflect on the morning's session.

My biggest worry was that Eric might not cooperate. If he continually created problems, it would seriously jeopardize Matt's ability to complete The Five-Day Turnaround.

I finished my notes for Day Two, packed up, and left.

The next morning, I arrived at the office early as usual. In all my years as an entrepreneur, I've been concerned about how I manage my day. I truly believe that time is our most valuable and scarce resource.

I have developed a Morning Ritual that serves me well:

Step One: Get Organized

For some, email can be a burden, but for me, the ease of communicating via email is a real plus. I can respond to things after thoughtful consideration (unlike text messages, which demand a prompt reply putting the message at risk of the medium). The first thing I do each morning is clear out my email inbox and check messages in other platforms (such as LinkedIn or Twitter) that might need a reply. I'm always more motivated and less distracted throughout the day when I start by clearing out the logjam of messages.

Step Two: Get Focused

Once I've cleared out my messages, I review my to-do list and calendar. My to-do list, which I keep in a notepad that I carry with me everywhere, keeps me focused on the essential things. I move the list to a new page each day, rewriting what remains. The discipline forces me to acknowledge which to-dos are the priority and which are less important. When I find myself rewriting a task several days in a row, it makes me reconsider whether it is imperative. The act of writing my to-dos also makes sure that I keep them top of mind.

My calendar is my daily and weekly playbook. I depend on color-coded entries to know exactly how I'm spending my time. Each morning, I look at the day ahead and the rest of the week. I make sure that my meetings make sense and that I have enough free time built in to respond to surprises that inevitably come up.

Step Three: Create "Headspace"

The third thing I address at the start of the day is what I call "Headspace." These are the handful of actions that are most important and need proactive time. As a leader, it can be easy to fall into the trap of reacting to the regular onslaught of seemingly urgent demands and distractions that land on your desk.

I keep my Headspace list in Evernote so I can review it on my phone, tablet, or laptop. Each proactive action is marked with a #headspace tag, allowing me to access the list quickly when needed. If the list grows too long, I question whether all of the things on it are truly important.

I finished my morning ritual and went to grab my first cup of coffee for the day. A few staff members had started to arrive. After saying good morning to them, I grabbed my laptop and notepad and went to one of the standing desks by the window.

As soon as I set up my laptop, I received a ping that I had a "priority" email. (I flag my most important contacts as priorities, so my notification system alerts me when they reach out to me.)

I pulled up the message:

Will,

Thanks again for the invigorating session yesterday. Here are some updates:

Eric grabbed me immediately after the meeting and complained again about the amount of time this would take. I reassured him that you know what you're doing, pointing to the years you spent as a top-notch business turnaround consultant at Ideathon. I told him he needed to trust me on this one.

We set up a meeting with the entire team for Wednesday morning to do the Values piece. Thanks for sending your suggestions yesterday afternoon. I'm going to use what you outlined in leading the session.

I grabbed some time with Eric and Meredith late yesterday afternoon. We were just touching base, but I started the time by reciting the PVTV (minus the Values, obviously). And, yes, it was awkward. But it made our conversation more productive! Next thing I'll do is memorize all of it.

Talk soon,
Matt

I replied:

Thanks. Let me know if I can help with Eric in any way, but my sense is he will join in at his own pace. And, yes, I do (kinda) know what I'm (kinda) doing. ;)

Glad you remembered to recite the PVTV! Looking forward to hearing how your Values building session goes on Wednesday.

Best,
Will

The one mission-critical component to all of this was for Matt to remain fully committed. So far, so good on that front.

Eric was another matter. At some point, he had to embrace the process, or he would have to leave the team. I actually wrote something to that effect in my initial email response to Matt but decided to delete it. He knew that is ultimately where this could end up. It was better to keep him focused on helping Eric see the light.

I was lost in thought about the Eric situation. Rachel brought me back to reality.

"Good morning, Will," she said. "How did your meeting go with Matt and his team?"

"Good morning back, Rachel," I said. "It was really good. We're making progress, and we've only just begun. I might be taking in more than I'm teaching, actually."

"Funny how that works, isn't it? They say the best way to learn a subject is to teach it."

I nodded. "So, Rachel, what's going on? Busy day today?"

"Always busy in operations," she said. "Have you been able to get a fix on the situation with RedBrick?"

"Nope, haven't," I said, realizing that so much time has gone into The Five-Day Turnaround with Matt that I hadn't given that situation much focus. I made a mental note to add it to my #headspace Evernote section. "What's your take on it?"

She took a deep breath, and I could tell she was being cautious. "To be honest, I'm quite concerned. You know how you get a gut feeling about something? We've been doing this long enough to sense a wrong turn, even if we can't put a finger on what it is. Something feels not quite right."

I considered her intuition. "Steve is a positive person," I said. "I think either he doesn't see the problem because he's too close to it, or he thinks it's a minor setback we'll overcome."

When working with clients, there are always issues that come up. A top-flight account manager can usually right the ship. They only raise a red flag when there's a dire emergency. Unfortunately, sometimes that happens too late.

I continued, "Can you pinpoint the thing that's causing you concern right now?"

"Yes. I'm sure you saw in the revenue projections that Steve has lowered RedBrick's billings for the quarter?" she replied, as much a question as a statement.

"Yes, I saw the numbers," I said.

"Well, they're asking for more team members to be working on the account! So we have a client that is reducing their spend with us but requiring more service at the same time. When I ask Steve why, he says it's the nature of the business, and they'll be back on track next quarter. I'm just not so sure," she said, shaking her head.

I paused for a moment to think. In the many years we'd worked with them, they'd never done that. "It's time to check in with Mark. We're overdue for a coffee anyway. He'll cue me in if there's a problem." Mark was the CMO of RedBrick and our first-line contact.

"That's a good call," she said. "In the meantime, what do you want me to do about allocating more team members to the account?"

"Work in some of the creative team's time over the next week, but keep it to a minimum until I meet with Mark." She said she could do that and headed back to her desk.

I jotted an email to Mark, asking for a meeting early next week. He responded almost immediately with a time on Tuesday afternoon. I sent him a calendar invite to lock in the time, color-coding it "green"—my color for client meetings.

I spent the rest of the day at the agency, before leaving around 5 p.m. to get a run in while it was still light outside.

Overall, the week was progressing well. As with every Wednesday morning, we had an all-hands meeting for thirty minutes where we reviewed how things were going against our goals. We acknowledged team members who have excelled at our Core Values. (It's great to see people get excited about recognizing their peers and being recognized by their peers.) To make things even better, our new business team had uncovered a few promising leads, and we got news that the agency was a finalist for a local award.

As the end of the day approached, I received a text from Matt that read:

> *Got a few minutes for me to update you on*
> *our Values meeting?*

I shot back:

> *You bet, let me know when I should call you.*

He answered:

> *Sending an overview via email with my notes.*
> *Call after reviewing.*

A few minutes later, I received his email.

Subject: Marketing Team Values
Trust in each other
Be comfortably uncomfortable
Argue, then commit
Be early

I was rather intrigued by what they had produced.

I gave Matt a ring, and he picked up almost immediately. I could tell he was charged up.

"Okay, what'd you think?" he asked.

"Well first off, I love that they're short and punchy and action-oriented. The fact that there are only four will help people remember them. Before you tell me more about each one, what was the process like getting to them?" I asked.

"It took a little bit of time to get people warmed up. But I took your advice and asked everyone to write down the characteristics they admire about their coworkers. I wrote those on Post-its and tacked them up," he said. "After that, I decided to ask what qualities they thought a winning sports team had. That got them more engaged."

"I love the metaphor of a sports team for a business team. Good thinking," I said.

"Working with those two inputs helped us land on those four values: 'Trust in each other,' 'Be comfortably uncomfortable,' 'Argue, then commit,' and 'Be early.' 'Trust in each other' is obvious, though I think it will be the most difficult of the four values to embrace totally," he said.

He was right. Trust takes time. It's hard to create and easy to break, but it is vital for a high-functioning team to be successful.

Matt continued, "'Be comfortably uncomfortable' was one that I didn't see coming. It stems from the need to thrive in a world of change and innovation. We had words like 'innovate' and 'think outside the box,' but I like 'comfortably uncomfortable.'

"'Argue, then commit' was a big one. We have to be comfortable sharing ideas that not everybody endorses. People have to get used to making a case for their point of view, especially to the boss. Once everyone has been heard, we can reach a decision. We have to be able to leave the room with all of us agreeing to support the decision, even if we didn't initially agree with it.

He continued, "I was really the one pushing for our final Value, 'Be early.' At first, this was about literally being early for meetings and deadlines. We tend to do things at the last minute, and I wanted to correct that behavior. But some people thought it implied being first with innovative ideas, early with products to market, and similar stuff. I LOVED the turn it took."

I laughed, "Awesome! I've found that a good Value is one with several angles to it. Do you believe everyone has bought into all four Values?"

"For now, I think the answer is yes," he replied. "We're going to work on ways to bring these values to life and make them a part of our decision-making process. Just like you said to do."

I laughed again. "Yes, the Values are going to be supportive only when they're operationalized. It's just like with the Purpose, Vision, and Tenets."

"Yep, okay. I gotta run, just wanted to make sure you knew where we landed. I owe you a call on Friday to share results for the rest of the week," he said.

We said goodbye and hung up. I was thrilled with his progress on the Values step. The most important aspect was having the team come up with their list together. I did not doubt that Matt would find ways to bring the Values to life and I'd be eager to hear about it on Friday.

α⌁o

When Friday finally arrived, I had a good call with Matt. He shared some significant progress from the week, and everything seemed on track.

So why was I feeling a sense that I was missing something? Was it going too smoothly?

After the call, I decided to head to The Steaming Cup to reflect on how far we had come and to prepare for tomorrow's meeting with Charles. We had agreed to meet at the park around the corner from my office. We would take a walk while catching up.

What was it that Matt had said? "This is way easier than I thought it would be! I think maybe we were ready for this change, and you gave us the push to get us over the edge."

That might be true, but I didn't think so.

And then it hit me.

Matt hadn't had to deal with constraints from the rest of the company yet. There had been no resistance, other than a few Eric tantrums along the way. I was sure it wouldn't take long for some conflict to develop with his peers in other departments. Their very different mindsets would infringe on his ability to move as fast and freely as a successful startup.

Admittedly, he was moving things along. During our call, he shared how he was bringing to life the Tenets and Values. He had organized his internal meeting agendas around the Tenets. It was a perfect way to put them into practice on a consistent basis.

He also made the Wi-Fi password "ComfortablyUncomfortable," which I thought was right on target. He said he planned to change it to another Value every few weeks, just to keep those beliefs top of mind.

Also, apparently on Thursday, there had been a big discussion within his team about the next quarter's campaigns. During the debate, one team member brought up the Tenet, "Maintain healthy partnerships." The group agreed that one of the options on the table could actually harm a key partnership. The group was able to coalesce around a different campaign. Matt said it was the first time he had seen the team work their way to a solution without him having to make a polarizing call.

He was doing the right things, but I wanted to see how he'd react when pushed by other parts of the business. Would he work his way out of it or would he fall into his old habit of conforming by slowing everything down?

I wouldn't have to wait long for the answer.

Saturday arrived bright and sunny. The park where I was meeting Charles was an inviting scene. The small lake was glistening with the morning sun, birds were singing their morning tunes, and there was a slight dew on the dark green grass that spread out along the 10-acre landscape.

I saw Charles heading into the park from its west end, riding his bike as usual. He came my way, waved, and parked. He greeted me happily as he locked up his bike. "What a glorious morning, my friend!"

"It doesn't get better than this, does it? Thanks again for meeting up. I hate to take any of your weekend time," I said.

"Don't be silly! We'll be walking outside in this beautiful park and getting some exercise, as well as talking about meeting a challenge—these are some of my favorite things to do," he reassured me.

We started walking the path that circled the park. Charles, already warmed up from his ride, was pushing us along at a brisk pace. His level of energy never ceased to amaze me, and I made a mental note to find more time in my weekly routine to work out more.

After briefing Charles on the week's events, he broke in, "Before we talk about your next Monday meeting with Matt, what are you most concerned about so far?"

This question had been on my mind, so I was ready with an answer. "I'm most concerned that it seems too easy. I'm not sure what I mean exactly, but I'd like Matt to be tested a little."

Charles laughed. "You know, the most successful leaders I've known are never satisfied when things are going well. They have a healthy amount of paranoia that keeps them out of danger. From my perspective, you are doing extremely well."

It was a relief to hear him say those words. Charles continued, "Remember, your biggest goal is to get Matt thinking like an entrepreneur. Whether he follows all of the rules, like implementing the Purpose, Vision, Tenets, and Values, at the end of the day the most important thing is his thinking like an entrepreneur. So far, that seems to be happening!"

He was right. That was happening. It hadn't taken very long for Matt to get his head in that space. Maybe it was because he'd worked in a startup before, but I sensed it was actually because he genuinely wanted to be a great leader and knew it was possible.

"Thanks for helping me see that more clearly," I said. "I expect there will be challenges at some point that will pressure-test all of this. My secondary concern is whether or not Eric will embrace this process. Matt really values him, and I know he's skilled at his craft..."

Charles cut in, "I actually think one of the best outcomes so far is Eric's skepticism."

A soccer ball that had escaped a young boy rolled onto the path in front of us, and Charles deftly stopped it and kicked it back to the child. He went on, "For one thing, you need the turnaround process pressure-tested since you've never done it before. Heck, I'm not sure anyone has tried to do this in just five days of meetings," he said. "You also need to prove that the process can win over negative people. His doubt is healthy, so long as he's not too rude in his delivery."

He was right, of course. I said, "Eric isn't too rude. Honestly, I told Matt something similar when we last spoke."

Changing gears, I said, "Okay, so on Monday we're at Day Three of Five—the midway point of the process. As you'll recall, that phase focuses on building trust within the team and creating an atmosphere to support it."

"Right! Matt will need to rethink his entire approach to the type of people he needs, what their strengths and weaknesses are... heck, what his entire structure should look like."

"Exactly!" I said.

We continued chatting as we circled the park a few times, recalling our past discussions on how teams build trust. Charles was such a wealth of information, and I was so glad to have him spend time with me.

After awhile, Charles and I agreed to grab an afternoon coffee next Friday, and then he hopped on his bike and headed off.

I sat down on a park bench to take in a little more of this beautiful morning and reflected on the role that mentors had played in my life.

My belief is, no matter who you are or what you're trying to accomplish, you can always use a good mentor. The question becomes, whom do you find and how do you want to work with them?

What has always surprised me is that smart people are usually very open to being a mentor. When I approached Charles so many years ago, I didn't truly know what I wanted the relationship to be. What I did know was that I was incredibly impressed by his insights and wanted to absorb whatever I could from his experience.

When I get the chance to talk to young, aspiring entrepreneurs and leaders, I always tell them to do two things: build your network and find some mentors. Those two drivers have helped grow my career as much as anything.

DAY THREE

It was Monday morning. Our third turnaround day. Matt and I were both at the office early. We grabbed a cup of coffee and made our way to the conference room. We exchanged the typical pleasantries, and then Matt said, "Before we start, I have to share something."

"You bet, what's up?" I asked.

"I know we're really just getting started here, but I already feel a change. Maybe it's just in my head, but I feel like, for the first time since I've been at Titan, that I'm managing my own team. Like, it's my own company within the larger company. I don't know if I'm explaining this right…" he trailed off.

"I think I get it," I said. "That is one of the hopeful outcomes. You start to realize that even though you're part of this larger business, in many ways, you can have your own team culture, marching to a faster-paced beat."

"Right! We still have to follow some routine for things that we've begun working on, and I know the hard work is yet to come, but already my approach is changing. I can see how well my team could function."

"In that spirit," I jumped in, "let's look at the third trait of successful startups. It's a key component of the entrepreneurial mindset."

I continued, "The title of today's maxim in The Five-Day Turnaround is: Trust in the Right People. It's got three major subsets."

"Got it," Matt said, jotting in his notebook. "Without the right resources, you'll never reach your goals."

"Ah, I'm so glad you said that. It brings me to my first point—words matter. How you refer to your team members is important. Personally, I always refer to mine as team members! I never refer to them as 'resources.' Have you ever looked up the meaning of the word 'resources'?"

"No, I guess not," he admitted.

"Lucky for you, I have," I smiled. "A resource is a stock or supply of money, materials, staff, or other assets that can be drawn on by a person or organization in order to function effectively."

"Ugh, yeah. I can see how that isn't exactly a great term for the people I count on each day."

"They may not even notice," I said. "They're used to a slow-moving company, to internal politics, and all the other things we're trying to change about your culture."

I continued, "Consider how they might feel if you started referring to them as 'team members.' That's a very different approach. A team member is defined as a person belonging to a specific group of people involved in attempting to achieve a common goal. Sounds different, doesn't it?"

"I get it, 100%. 'Team members' are a group of individuals working together to achieve a common goal. 'Resources' are people that I use to achieve what I want." He shook his head. "It's team members from now on."

"Great," I said and handed Matt one of the whiteboard markers. "Now, let's get to it. I'd like you to start a list on the board. Call it 'Reasons Hired,' and put a 1–5 number listing underneath it."

He got up and wrote on the whiteboard:

Reasons Hired:

1.
2.
3.
4.
5.

"Now, think about the reasons you've hired people for your team. Find the five most common attributes you look for and write them up there," I said.

Matt said, "Easy." He filled out the list rather quickly.

Reasons Hired:

1. Industry experience
2. Great education
3. Impressive application
4. Brought new skill to the team
5. ~~**Laughed at my jokes**~~ **Great personality**

I laughed when he filled in number five.

"Okay. Now to the right of that list, start another one. Call it 'Our Values' and write your team values underneath in a similar fashion," I said.

He completed the board, having to refer to his notes a few times to get the Values correct.

Reasons Hired:

1. Industry experience
2. Great education
3. Impressive application
4. Brought new skill to the team
5. ~~**Laughed at my jokes**~~ **Great personality**

Our Values

1. **Trust in each other**
2. **Be comfortably uncomfortable**
3. **Argue, then commit**
4. **Be early**

Matt stepped away from the whiteboard and looked at me for input. I asked, "Do you see any problem with this?"

He looked back at the whiteboard and said, "Uh...not really."

I got up, grabbed a red marker, and wrote:

Nice to Have

Reasons Hired:

1. **Industry experience**
2. **Great education**
3. **Impressive application**
4. **Brought new skill to the team**
5. ~~**Laughed at my jokes**~~ **Great personality**

Must Have

Our Values

1. **Trust in each other**
2. **Be comfortably uncomfortable**
3. **Argue, then commit**
4. **Be early**

I walked back to my seat and sat down, letting Matt digest what I had written.

"You can't be suggesting that it's more important for me to hire people who have our Values than it is to hire someone with great experience." Matt was incredulous.

"I sure am," I said.

"That's crazy, nobody hires that way," he said.

"Ah, see that's where you're wrong. Most people don't hire like that, I'll admit. And almost all established corporations don't do it. But when you talk to startups, the really successful ones, they hire first on Culture Fit and Values every time," I replied.

"I don't know…." He shook his head slowly.

I continued, "Remember Misty back at Crackersnap?"

"Of course! She was the head of operations. Terrific, totally reliable. She saved us from countless disasters," he said.

"She sure did. Do you remember her first job with us, when we were just getting started?" I asked.

"I think she was the office manager, right?"

"That's right. Tell me, what are a few of the qualities you thought made her indispensable," I said.

"She was always positive and enthusiastic…when she said she'd do something, she always got it done…and she was always honest. Sometimes brutally, but she always talked straight," he said.

"So Misty had all of these qualities when she started at Crackersnap, and she did a great job at operations. She moved up the company ladder each year until she was on the leadership team," I said.

"Now, was it her resume, her…" I looked up at the whiteboard, "…great education, the new skills she brought to the team, that helped her rise? Or was it the Values you just described that were inherent in who she was?"

He sat back in his chair and smiled at me. "Okay, okay, I was wrong. Yes, of course, it was Misty's Values and who she was. She learned operations while there, and likely was successful in her role because of her inherent attributes."

"And she probably would have been a winner at anything she was asked to do," I added.

"Agreed. So you're saying I should be hiring against our team Values rather than anything else?" he asked.

"Absolutely, and…" I paused for a brief second, "…you should re-evaluate all of your team members against these Values. If you believe that any of them are never going to fit in, they should be asked to leave."

He put his head in his hands and then looked up at me, eyes squinting with feigned pain. "I was afraid you'd say something like that. I have already gone through that process with Eric and Meredith. I matched our four Values against each of them."

"And how did that go?" I asked, very curious.

"You might be surprised, but Eric actually fit with the Values fairly well. He has to get better about 'Trust in Each Other,' but I can work with him on that. With Meredith, as you know, she's great in so many ways, but I worry that she won't be able to 'Argue, then Commit.' I do need her to be confident enough to disagree with me, or anyone on the team, when she feels strongly about something. Again, I think I can help her with that, but it's a concern."

"Based on my limited interactions with them, I think you're probably spot-on. So for now, they both pass?" I asked.

"They do, thankfully. So what do you think about me working with the two of them to assess the rest of the team?" he asked.

"I think that works. What I'd do is create three categories. One for 'Yes' team members, another for 'Yes, but needs work,' and another for 'No.' Be ready. Making choices will be tough. With the size team you have, I'll be surprised if at least a few people aren't a match."

"Okay, what's the next step in the process? You said there were three, I assume hiring on Values versus Experience was #1?" he wondered.

"That's right; you nailed it. So once your hiring is centered on Values, the second thing you have to do is make sure you have The Right People, in the Right Position, at the Right Time," I said.

"Right people...right position...right time..." he said, writing in his notebook.

"What we have to combat," I said, "is team members who were right in their role at first but end up in the wrong position as the company's needs changed or they've fallen victim to the Peter Principle."

Matt shook his head. "Explain this one. What's the Peter Principle?" he asked.

"The Peter Principle is a classic. It says that a person will rise in a company to the level of their incompetence," I said.

"How's that again?" he asked.

"Think of it like this. You have a great graphic designer. She is doing terrific work, so you promote her. Now she's an Art Director, responsible for the creative for full campaigns. She struggles a little at first but gains her footing. Ultimately, she's great at creating the overall campaign strategies. She's doing so well, in fact, that you promote her again, this time to Creative Director, where her responsibility is not just to make sure that the artwork is outstanding, but also that each member of the creative team is performing well. She's now managing a highly imaginative group of people. With me so far?" I ask.

"Yep, sounds like the typical path," he said.

"And so here's the kicker, she's not a great manager of people. Turns out, she's an impressive sole contributor, but she's not made for managing others. She doesn't like conflict, and she has a hard time delegating. Ultimately, she's just a bad manager. So what happens?" I ask.

"That's a tough one. I guess I'd wonder what happened and hope she'd figure it out," he said.

"And how long would you give her to get it all figured out?" I asked.

"Heck, maybe forever. I'd always think she was about to sort it out because she had always succeeded in the past."

"Exactly. That's the Peter Principle. People keep getting promoted until they find themselves in a position not suitable for their strengths, and that's where they stay. They go from being a reliable team member to being a detriment to the team. They're not happy with what they are doing, and the team suffers. Big companies are notorious for incompetence caused by the Peter Principle." I paused. "Ya know which type of business does not have this problem?"

Matt smiled. "Let me guess... successful startups?"

"Right you are," I said. "Even if people aren't Peter Principled, they still need to be in the right position at the right time. You're changing your culture to be agile and fast-moving. It's likely you could find that you have a team member in the right position today who isn't a great fit six months from now, not because they have changed for the worse, but because your environment has transformed."

Matt nodded his head. "Got it," he said.

"There's one exercise I want you to do. You can do this with Eric and Meredith if you like, or on your own. Map out the organizational structure that you'd create if you were starting from scratch. As if today was the first day on the job. What roles do you need? What structure makes the most sense? What current roles do you have now that need to be changed or completely removed?" I asked. "Those are things you need to figure out this week and report back to me."

He was making notes in his notepad, then looked up and said, "Will do."

"Cool, now let's go for a walk. Let's slowly walk through your office. It's…" I looked at my phone to get the time. "11:15 a.m., perfect. Let's just stroll through. Observe as much as you can, then we'll come back, and I'll ask you a few questions."

"Okay, sounds good. Just follow me," Matt said.

We walked out of the conference room and started to wind our way through his department. There were many conference rooms. The team members who weren't in a conference room were quietly working in their high-walled cubes. We passed Eric's office and Meredith's office. Eric had positioned his desk so he was facing away from the door, but Meredith was facing out, and she gave us a big wave as we walked by.

We made our way back to our meeting room and sat down. "Okay, tell me what you observed," I said.

"Well, I'll admit it's not very startup-y," he said.

"How do you mean?" I asked.

"Well, you guys always have your skateboards out and music playing, and sometimes you even have dogs running around! We can't operate like that. What we're doing is too serious," he said.

"Right," I said. "What you're doing is serious. What happens if your department doesn't look like it will hit its numbers this quarter?"

"Hmm. I suppose I might have to make a few cuts to make up for it next quarter?" he said.

"Right. If a startup has a bad quarter, they might go out of business. So remind me again which group should be more 'serious'?" I asked, unsuccessfully hiding my sarcasm.

"Yeah, okay, but this is a…" he paused.

"A what?" I asked.

"Well, I was going to say a 'legacy corporation,' but then I realized how ridiculous that would sound because it's what we're here fighting against!" he said.

I couldn't help but laugh. "What else did you notice?"

"I don't know. Everything we saw was very normal to me," he said.

I wanted to push him on this, so I said, "Think about the setup at Crackersnap. Any differences?"

"Well, there were no cubes, probably because we couldn't afford them at first," he said.

"True, but over time, even when we could afford cubes, we never bought them. Maybe that's just because we were used to it, but we had great communication and trust. I think a part of that was because fewer walls separated us, figuratively and literally."

"I can see that," he said. "And now that I think about it, it seems like most of the startups I've visited, yours included, have whiteboards all over the place and people meeting at them, out in the open. We definitely don't have that here."

"Absolutely," I agreed. "I've taken that lesson forward in my company and embraced a more open and collaborative environment." I checked the time. "And now it's time for you to head to your next meeting," I said with a smile.

"What meeting is that?" he asked, with a curious expression on his face.

"Oh, I didn't tell you?" I asked coyly. "I set you up to visit my friend Rob Daniels for a half hour at his office at noon. I was there recently and realized his environment is the polar opposite of yours. I thought it would be good for you to see it and hear his logic behind it. The meeting should already be in your calendar. I had your admin add it this morning."

"Rob Daniels, the CEO of Friendly People? We use their software. I'd love to meet him!" Matt was excited.

"Great! You need to head over there now. I also took the liberty of asking if you could meet me Saturday morning here, at your office. Your admin said your calendar is open."

Matt looked skeptical, so I continued cautiously, "I need you to trust me here. I want you to ask your team members to pack up all of their stuff in their cubes—equipment and everything. Put it into boxes that I'll have delivered before they leave on Friday."

"Oh boy, here we go. Okay, Will. I trust you. I'm on this journey, so I might as well play it out. Just make sure the boxes are here, and I'll get the team to pack up their stuff. They'll probably think I'm firing them all!" he said.

"Just tell them there is some remodeling happening in the office this weekend. It'll be fine," I said, packing up my stuff.

We headed out of the conference room and went on our separate ways. Matt went to Rob's office, and I went to mine. Matt wasn't the only one with a big week ahead of him. I was meeting with Mark, the CMO of RedBrick, tomorrow, and I needed to prep.

Yesterday's meeting with Matt had gone really well, and I was more confident than ever that genuine change was starting to take hold. I had moved beyond the point of worrying about whether my agency would win the business. My focus was on helping Matt and his team make a successful transformation!

My Tuesday morning was on track. Up early, first cup of coffee at the office, Morning Ritual done—and then I got the email update from Matt.

Will,

I'll be honest. I had a fitful night's sleep. I'm sure I'll have to rethink what works and what doesn't for my team after our meeting yesterday. Obviously, I've let people go before, but always for a specific reason. "You don't fit our culture" will be a tough one for me. I've set up a time to meet with HR to discuss.

Otherwise, the rest of yesterday progressed according to plan. The meeting with Rob Daniels BLEW ME AWAY. I want to be him, and I want to learn from observing his culture. Not really, but kinda. :) I have a list of to-do notes on what I saw.

One thing I have to share. Yesterday afternoon the CEO came into my office, and he was holding one of the PVTV postcards I made for all my team members. Did I tell you I did that? Anyway, he said he found it on someone's desk and asked me if I was having a mid-life crisis or something! His exact words were, "You aren't going all Jerry Maguire on me, are you?" Which is funny, because that is one of my favorite movies and, yes, I do kind of feel like that.

Anyway, he was aware of something unusual. He told me to 'keep my eye on the ball,' which of course I will.

Okay, big week, gotta run.
Matt

I replied:

I love that you made PVTV postcards, and no, you didn't tell me. Keep an eye out for your CEO. I expect that after this weekend, he might make another trip to your office. ;)

Re: Keep your notes from the meeting with Rob at Friendly People until we meet up on Saturday morning.

Best,
Will

After I hit send, I remembered my conversation with Shera a few weeks back. She had mentioned that positive internal politics and quick wins would be necessary for a program like this to succeed. For Matt to give this a solid effort, he'd need his CEO and his peer group to support him in various ways.

I quickly typed up another email:

Matt,

One more thing. In preparation for our meeting next Monday, write a list of your peers. Include your CEO. Rate them on a scale of 1-10, with ten being "marvelous" and one being "terrible" in describing your relationship with them.

For instance, if the head of HR is someone that trusts you entirely and will support whatever matters to you, that's a ten. If the head of finance hates your guts and will throw you under the bus given a chance, that's a one.

Just write a simple list and ratings, and we'll talk on Monday.

Best,
Will

Knowing Matt, I was pretty sure he'd be handing out many high ratings. He was a very personable guy and knew how to win people over. Still, he'd need real support to pull this off, and some quick wins too.

Just then, Steve walked up and said, "Boss, you headed to RedBrick soon?"

Checking my phone for the time, I realized it was indeed time for me to head over there. "Yep, leaving now. I'll let you know how it goes!"

"Thanks. Remember, Mark recently had a second child. A little girl. We sent a big care package," he said.

"Great tip," I said, as I headed out the door.

RedBrick was a company whose office building lived up to its name. Just off the interstate, it rose up 25 floors and was made entirely of Georgia red brick.

I had a chance once to see the founder of RedBrick give a talk at a conference. He spoke about how, as an entrepreneur, you're going to be the target of a brick or two along the way. He said, "It's in those moments when you can decide whether that blow will knock you down and out of the game, or if you can catch the brick and use it to build the foundation of your business. That's what I decided to do, and it's why I ultimately decided to have a brick in my company name."

He then pointed up to his hair—he had a thick, somewhat unruly stock of red hair—and said, "And the 'red' is for, well, this."

I always remembered that speech and referred to it as the "Catching Bricks" talk. It was a lesson that I took to heart in building my company, trying to take each challenging situation, each bit of bad news, each "how can we recover from this" blow and use it to make my company stronger.

The talk came to mind as I waited in the lobby for Mark. His assistant came to get me and took me up the elevator to the top floor where all the executives had offices. We made our way to Mark's office. It was one of the corner offices and was set up with a separate meeting room connected to his workspace.

She sat me down in the meeting room and asked if I needed water or a coffee. I almost always accept the offer of a glass of water as you never know how long the discussion will go.

Mark came in a few minutes later, apologizing for being a few minutes late. He asked how I've been.

"Things are going really well. The company is growing, and the family is good. That reminds me! Congratulations to you on your newest addition! I brought you a little something," I said.

I reached into my bag and pulled out a little pink onesie with my agency's logo on the front. Under the logo, it said, "Intern."

He loved the gift, laughing and calling his assistant in to see it. "Thanks for the thoughtfulness. I'll be sure to send you a photo of her wearing it when she's big enough."

I reflected on how different Mark was from Matt. Mark was older and had been a CMO for much longer. He was always dressed very professionally, often in a suit and tie. You'd describe him as more "old school" based on how he managed, but I also found him to be a thoughtful and personable leader, which I very much respected.

After exchanging more pleasantries, I got down to business.

"Mark, thanks again for taking the time to meet up. I wanted to check in and see how things are going with the agency relationship. You know you can be straight with me, and I always appreciate your feedback," I said.

"Things are good. Our teams work so well together, sometimes I feel like they're one and the same team, actually," he said. "It's hard to find a dependable agency partner, so I value how well our people jell."

I was hearing the words "good" and "dependable"—not "great" which was what I was hoping to get from him.

I pushed a little further. "That's nice to hear. Obviously, our team loves working with you guys too. What about Steve, how's he doing lately? Please, remember, you can be honest."

"Steve's the best. I don't think I've ever worked with an agency account leader as responsive and well-liked as Steve. He's always very positive and upbeat," Mark said. I decided not to respond straight away, giving him a minute to see if he'd add anything. Luckily, he did. "I've told Steve he can tell me if there's anything I can do to help you guys do a better job and he always says there isn't. I have to think there is, and maybe he doesn't want to upset me or something."

Now we were getting somewhere. Mark wouldn't say that to Steve if he thought things were stupendous.

"You know, you're probably right. Steve's a guy who would want to be careful not to offend you. I can talk to him about that. Is there something specific you're hoping he might address?" I asked.

He sat back in his chair and thought for a moment. "No, I can't say that there is at the moment. I guess I just feel like we're repeating the same thing all the time. Nothing truly surprising is happening with our marketing efforts. I'm not sure if that's a bad thing. Our results are still outdistancing the competition," he said.

He was about to say more when his assistant came in and politely said, "I'm sorry to bother you all, but Mark, I just received a note from Barbara, and she needs you immediately." Barbara was the CEO, so Mark immediately jumped up.

"Ah, sorry Will, I have to go. Thanks again for coming in. As I said, I think things are fine. Sorry we didn't have more time to talk."

I was disappointed that we were ending the conversation before I could get to the root of what was bothering him.

Mark's assistant walked me to the exit. I sat in my car and made some notes in my notebook. I always made sure to capture meeting notes while the session was going on or immediately after to be sure I didn't miss anything.

I'd confirmed the feeling that something was not right, but I still couldn't quite put my finger on it. Thank goodness I knew just whom to ask for advice.

It was Friday. I had spent the rest of the week making good progress on many fronts, but I still hadn't nailed what was going on with RedBrick...or for that matter, if anything was going on. It sure seemed that something was amiss. I had confirmed that the CMO wasn't thrilled and there still were red flags at the agency about needing more team members on the account.

Thankfully, I was meeting with Charles this afternoon, and I was pretty sure he'd be able to help me figure this one out.

Meanwhile, Matt and I had agreed to have a call at 10 a.m. to recap how the rest of the week had progressed. I was eager to hear what he had to say. I dialed his line, and he picked up quickly.

"Will, how're things?" he said.

"Pretty good, how's it been over there? Did you buy a convertible to go with your mid-life crisis?" I joked.

He laughed. "No, not yet. But I'll think about it, let me add that to my to-do list…" He paused for dramatic effect. "Got it, 'Buy a red convertible.'"

I laughed. "Nice. So tell me, what's been happening this week?"

"It's been interesting," he said. "I spent a lot of time thinking about the team overall and what structure would be right if I were to start from scratch."

"Did you invite Eric and Meredith into the process?" I asked.

"I did, after going through it on my own," he said. "We spent time first talking about our Purpose, Vision, Tenets, and Values…"

"Yep, exactly as you should, to help shape the conversation," I interjected.

"Exactly. I knew you'd appreciate that one," Matt said. "And then I asked them, 'Based on those Values, what kind of organizational structure do we need? What kind of people, in what roles, would make the most sense?' It was hard for them to free their minds from what we are today, but I think we finally got through it."

"And where did you end up?" I asked.

"Well, most of the changes came from the idea that we shouldn't focus on 'marketing,' we should focus on growth. That was the biggest mind shift that we went through. After realizing this, everything kind of flowed nicely. That is until Eric changed everything," he said.

Now I was curious. "What do you mean, he changed everything?"

"You know Eric. He was being his usual, cynical self. He said that none of this made sense because I was the Chief Marketing Officer, not the Chief Growth Officer. That was a tough one to argue with," he said.

"How did you respond?" I asked.

He chuckled and said, "Well, I couldn't argue with the point so I told him he was right, that my title should be Chief Growth Officer. So I changed that on the whiteboard where we were redesigning the org chart. I crossed out 'Marketing' and wrote, 'Growth.'"

"So are you going to talk to the CEO about changing your title?" I asked, uncertain about how this line of thinking might go.

"You bet I did. I set up a meeting to discuss it this afternoon," Matt said. "We'll see how it goes. My boss already thinks I'm getting a bit loony. There's no telling how he will react. I think if I stress that this will help my team focus on the bottom line growth of the business, he might go for it."

As I mentioned previously to Matt when he referred to his team members as "resources," words are important. Changing his title to Chief Growth Officer would signify a big plus for the team.

"So did you end up changing the structure of your team, and were there any roles or people that need to be replaced?" I asked.

"Yes, and I want to say 'unfortunately,' but I know it's for the better. We realized that we had two roles not needed any longer, and two new roles we'd need to hire," he said.

"And we have a few team members that just won't be able to make the transition, so we'll need some changes there," he continued. "I have already met with HR and started talking about the steps we'll need to take."

Matt was moving incredibly fast, much faster than I expected. His old startup self must be kicking in.

"Man, you're truly committed to this!" I said. "How are you feeling?"

"That's just it...before we started the turnaround, I would have been very nervous about all of these changes. Who would I upset? What would my peers think? On and on. Then I realized that none of that matters if I'm not delivering 100% toward the growth of the company. Once that became the clear goal, everything has become easier to do," Matt said.

He continued, "But wow, are people freaked out right now about having to pack up their desks. I've told them not to worry, but, as you know, change is always disconcerting."

"Yes, that's one of the things that will be different soon. We want people to embrace and celebrate change, rather than run from it. Some of your folks might not be able to adjust, but I think most will. When actions lead to success, everyone usually gets on board," I said.

"Okay, well, I guess I'll see you bright and early tomorrow morning," he said.

"You bet, see you then!" I said, enthusiastically.

We hung up, and I was thrilled about the progress Matt was making. Hopefully tomorrow morning he'd buy into our most daring move yet.

I sat in one of the small conference rooms at our office for my phone call with Charles.

"Will, how are you?" Charles said, practically shouting. I could tell he was driving and using his Bluetooth.

"Never better," I said, matching his enthusiasm. "How about you?"

"Terrific. It's just one glorious day after another. You know, I could get used to this retirement thing," he replied.

"Ha, from what I can tell, you're still working 40 hours or more a week with all the consulting and nonprofit work you're doing. I'm not sure many people would call it 'retirement,'" I said.

"True, true, but when you love what you do, it never feels like work. Speaking of which, catch me up on the journey with Matt," he prompted.

I walked him through the week, making sure to hit all the high spots. When I got to the part about Matt wanting to change his title to Chief Growth Officer, Charles broke in. "How about that! It came from the naysayer! I once did a title change myself. Have I ever told you about it?" he asked.

"No, I don't think you have. You changed your title?"

"Yes, it was at a time when my company was having some culture problems, and I wanted everyone to know that I was doubling down on the importance of our staff members. I changed my title to Chief People Officer," he said.

"What? You changed from CEO to Chief People Officer?" I asked in amazement.

"I did! And it was one of the smartest things I could have done. When everyone saw I was willing to shed the title of CEO, they knew I was putting my ego aside and putting our people first. Little did they know, I never much liked the title of CEO anyway," he said, with a chuckle.

Classic Charles.

"That's fantastic," I said, then shifted gears. "Charles, I appreciate you making the time on a Friday afternoon. The main reason I wanted to chat with you is to get your advice on something I'm dealing with at my agency," I said.

I walked him through the RedBrick situation. He listened quietly until I finished.

"Let's start with this—what does your gut say is happening?" Charles asked.

"That's just it. I can't put my finger on it. My gut does say something is out of whack but I don't know what, and I don't know how severe it is," I said.

"It's clear something is going on. Otherwise, you wouldn't be worried about it. You're experienced enough to read the signals," he assured.

I knew exactly what he meant.

He continued, "Are you in front of your computer?"

"Yep."

"Can you access your agency time entries to tell how much attention a client gets?" he asked.

"You bet," I replied, opening up our time tracking software.

"Good. Here is what I'm wondering. Look at the last three months of RedBrick, and tell me how many hours get spent on creative versus time in meetings. Can you access that?" he asked.

"Definitely," I said, clicking through the various reports that the program creates. "Found it. Over the last three months, looking at percentages...okay, we've spent..." I stopped, perplexed. "Wait, that can't be right."

"What does it say?" he asked.

"It says we spent 40% of our time in meetings and only 15% on creative," I said, astonished. "But that can't possibly be correct."

"Run the report against the first three months working with the account and let's see. Presuming the team doesn't enter their time differently now versus then..."

"...they don't," I added.

"...it should look comparable," he finished.

I did as he suggested and sure enough, there was a huge discrepancy. "It says that the first three months of the relationship, we spent almost 50% of our time on creative and less than 20% in meetings."

He didn't say anything, letting me ponder what the reading conveyed.

"Wow, no wonder Mark seemed frustrated because we aren't exciting them with new ideas these days. I get why Steve is eager to have more help. The creatives are in meetings all the time!" I said, almost shouting.

"Why do you think there are so many meetings?" he asked.

I thought about it, but I couldn't come up with a good answer. "I honestly don't know. What do you think, Charles?"

"Well, typically when meetings grow in frequency and length, it's because there is a lack of trust among the team members," he said.

"Lack of trust?" I asked, not believing that could be the reason. "But we work hard at our company to communicate openly and break down walls."

"It's true you've done many things to make trust a priority. We've talked about that before. The blog post you wrote last year about the benefits of an open floor plan is one of my favorites. I've passed it on to several friends as a way to begin building trust," he said.

He continued, "Consider that maybe your company as a whole has a high level of trust with you and your leadership, but the RedBrick team might be functioning differently within their own ecosystem. When people become distrusting, when they worry they aren't being treated fairly, when they feel like their voice isn't heard, when there's backstabbing and finger-pointing, calling for more meetings is usually the result. People create meetings to provide cover."

I built on his thinking, "And more meetings creates a slower moving, less nimble organization." I shook my head. "Jeez. That's exactly what I'm trying to help Matt fight! I suppose I should be drinking my own Kool-Aid on this one."

"Sounds likely, my friend. Don't be too hard on yourself. It's an easy trap. The good news is I think maybe you've caught what's happening early enough to turn the ship around," he said.

We talked for another 15 minutes, and by the end of our conversation I had a solid list of things to discuss with the team on Monday. I sent an email invitation to Steve and the entire RedBrick team for that afternoon, calling it: "This is not a meeting."

Matt and I pulled into the Titan parking lot on Saturday morning at the same time. We were both ten minutes early for our 9 a.m. meeting.

"I still can't beat you to a meeting!" I laughed as we shook hands.

"You almost did today. So, what are we doing here on a weekend? We should be home with our kids."

"True. We wouldn't be doing this if it wasn't important," I said. "I'll explain everything over a cup of coffee. You do know how to work the coffee machines in this place, don't you?"

He laughed. "Of course. I took 'Coffee Machine Management 101' at Harvard B School."

It took some time, but Matt did indeed figure out how to work the machine. We got our coffees and had a seat in the glass-walled conference room that overlooks his department.

"Do you remember your visit to see Rob at Friendly People?" I asked.

"Of course. Loved it," he said.

I pointed beyond the conference room glass wall toward his department's mass of cubes and smiled.

"Oh hold on now. You want us to change my department to be like Rob's office?" he shot back, knowing very well that's what I intended but still not believing it.

"You bet I do. See those cubes? They need to come down completely. We are going to put people with offices out in the open. We're going to convert their offices to small breakout and conference rooms. We'll put whiteboard paint on that wall over there and add open meeting areas there, there, and there," I said, pointing to several different places around the room.

Matt was looking at me wide-eyed.

"I have a blueprint for you right here," I said, and pulled out the plan.

"You have a blueprint?" Matt was shocked.

I nodded, smiling.

He shook his head. "Still. Even if we could do all of this today—which I'm sure we can't—and even if we had the new office furniture—which I'm sure we don't—I can't imagine my COO will be happy with me coming in here and changing our entire department without consulting him first."

"Assuming I can take care of the first two roadblocks, what's the worst thing that would happen if your COO came in on Monday and saw the changes?" I asked.

"Well, he'd be mad, probably mostly because I didn't run it by him beforehand," Matt paused and looked thoughtful. "Of course, he did approve the legal team redoing their area a few months back. Fact is, they didn't do much, and it was very 'attorney-like.' What you're suggesting is very…"

"…startup-like?" I suggested.

"...yeah, sure, startup-like. I don't think he's going to be too keen on it," Matt said.

"Well, in my experience, it's better to ask forgiveness rather than permission, especially when you're fighting against the status quo. The main thing is, can your relationship with the COO take the hit? Have you built up enough trust to pull this off and gain his forgiveness?" I asked.

He thought for a minute and said, "Yeah, for sure I have. I didn't know I'd be cashing it all in so soon, but I've helped him out enough times. I think he'll have my back. So, if I'm willing to take on the risk, how do you suggest all of this happens?"

I smiled wide and said, "Let's go back out to the parking lot for a minute."

We walked back outside where there was a truck, a portable storage unit, and eight men waiting for us.

"Matt, this is a moving team that I have helping us today. In that truck is all of the IKEA furniture and supplies you saw listed on the blueprint." Pointing, I said, "That storage unit is where we're going to put all of your existing furniture for safekeeping."

Matt was stunned. He looked at me, wide-eyed. "How...? When...?"

I laughed. "Don't worry about the cost. I already have a buyer who is ready to purchase your existing furniture for the exact cost of everything I purchased to replace it. An even swap, basically."

"Wow, I don't know what to say," he said.

"How about, 'Let's get started'!" I said.

Matt nodded. He was getting excited. "Okay, yep, why the heck not?"

Over the next eight hours, everybody worked hard. All of the old furniture was moved out, and Matt and I put together countless desks, tables, chairs, couches, and even a few standing desks.

We arranged the desks according to the new organizational changes, and we set up the couches for small meeting areas next to the windows. No one would have a personal office, and no one would have a preferred place to sit.

No one, that was, except for Matt. I was still having trouble convincing him to give up his office. In fact, he hadn't packed up his office.

"Matt, think about it. You don't want to be the one person who doesn't accept this new way of being, do you?" I asked.

"But I need an office! I'm constantly in meetings or have to make private phone calls. Sometimes I need space to think. Plus it's all set up nicely..."

I jumped in, "You can still have all of that without having your own office. There are plenty of meeting spaces we've created. We could make your office a special meeting room and only allow your admin to reserve it. That way, if you need privacy, it will always be available. This change is cultural. It won't work if you're not part of it."

"Plus," I said, "when I made the same change, moving out into the open, I was more aware of what was happening and more in tune with our culture. I showed everyone that I was one of them and that I had nothing to hide. That was five years ago. I can't see ever having my own office again."

It took another 15 minutes, but Matt finally acquiesced. He said he'd "give it a try." I took the confirmation and ran with it. He spent about an hour packing his stuff, while I continued putting together IKEA furniture. When Matt finished, he called me into his office.

He had two piles of boxes and, pointing to the much larger one, said, "So what do I do with all of this stuff?"

The pile he pointed to had all of his knick-knacks, photos, and awards. There was no way for that stuff to fit on his new desk in the open area.

I smiled and said, "Good thing you didn't get that little convertible yet. How big is your car trunk?"

We continued working for the rest of the afternoon. We had pizzas and sodas delivered for everyone. I tried to buy beer for the crew, but Matt said something about liability, so I decided to let him have a win on that one.

The last thing to be done was to apply whiteboard paint on a large wall. Several of the guys were working on that task. Matt and I sat, exhausted, and watched them for a moment.

"So, I talked to the CEO on Friday about changing my title to Chief Growth Officer," he said.

"Really? How did that go?" I asked.

"He wasn't convinced at first, so I talked him through why the change made sense. I explained how it would enable me to lead my team more effectively in the company rather than simply 'marketing our brand.' He had two concerns. One was that I might hurt myself with my next job because companies weren't really hiring Chief Growth Officers frequently. The other was that it might cause a conflict with Ann, our head of Sales."

"Fair points," I said.

"Fair, but I'd already considered both objections. In fact, I had talked to Ann first to get her blessing. She took a little convincing too, but I assured her the nature of my role wouldn't change and that one of my big initiatives was to begin working more closely with her team to make them more successful. That did the trick," he said.

"And what about his point about your career?" I asked.

He smiled, "I told him my goal is to be so good at what I do that companies will be fighting to hire me no matter what my title was."

"Now that's real confidence!" I congratulated him. "Well done!"

"Thanks! So I'll need to work with HR to make the necessary adjustments in my team. Then I'll announce my title change. I'll shoot for the middle of next week for that. Of course, I'll also have to explain this new office layout to everyone. They'll all see the redesign when they get in on Monday..." Matt paused, mentally reviewing his calendar. "Wait, you and I are planning to meet on Monday morning...I really think I need to be here when they arrive."

He was right. I hadn't thought of that either. "How about we move our meeting to Wednesday morning instead?"

We both checked and the timing was available, so I changed the calendar invite.

When everything was done, and the movers took the truck and the storage unit away, we did a few laps around the new space. It was a complete 180-degree change from his previous setup. We stopped only at removing the carpet to expose the hardwood floors underneath; we decided that might be taking things too far.

As we came to a stop near his new desk, Matt observed, "I gotta say, this feels really good to me. We'll feel more like a team out here. But I'm sure people are going to freak out, especially the folks that we moved out of a personal office," he said.

"In my experience, some people will be freaked. But in a few weeks, they'll be used to it, and almost everyone will see the benefit of the change."

We said our goodbyes and hit the road for home. I was relieved to have pushed back our next meeting to Wednesday. There was planning to do for the RedBrick team meeting on Monday.

Steve had sent me several messages since I sent out the invite to the team. I told him not to worry and to be open-minded and honest when we did meet. This response only caused him to send more messages. I finally replied by telling him he'd have to wait until Monday. I needed him to be raw in the meeting and did not want to give him time to have well-rehearsed responses. I was searching for honesty, not perfection, which I thought was part of our overall issue.

"Okay, you're probably wondering what this meeting is about," I said to the RedBrick team. It was Monday afternoon, and I had been anticipating the session all day.

"Especially," I continued, "because I named the meeting, '*This is not a meeting.*'"

A few nervous laughs bubbled up from the team of about 20. This group had grown so much over the years. I was proud of them, but it was time to rebuild their structure to reflect the type of organization we needed to be—fast, scrappy, and creative.

"I'm going to start by asking a tough question. I want to stress that we need honesty today. We're all here because we want to be a great partner to RedBrick, and the only way we'll make sure that continues to happen is if we can be frank with each other," I paused. "So, the question I'd like you to think about is this. If we were to lose RedBrick, what would have been the reason?"

This type of question has been a useful tool for me in business. I have often posed a similar challenge to my leadership team: If we were to go out of business, what would be the reason? This line of thinking helps them crystallize what concerns them most. I've found that game-changing ideas can come from going down this uncomfortable path and I was hoping for some of that kind of thinking to surface this afternoon.

I looked at the group and asked, "Okay, who's first?"

Brian, one of the creatives on the team, raised his hand and said, "Because we disappointed them."

"How so?" I asked.

"I guess I mean, we came up with ideas they didn't care for?" he replied, more asking a question than making a statement.

I looked around the room. "Can anyone build on what Brian is suggesting?"

"Sure, I think I can," said Carla. Carla led the strategy unit of the team. "If we consistently give them creative ideas or even strategic concepts that they deem below their expectations, they might decide to use another agency."

Jessica, Steve's top account person on the team, added, "That would probably happen if they saw bad results due to the work, right? I believe they trust us enough not to judge our work based on their feelings, but if our campaigns don't perform in the marketplace, then we're toast."

I saw several heads nodding at this point, so I asked, "How did the last campaign perform?"

No one spoke up. Finally, Steve answered, "They said it did quite well, but I don't have any actual numbers."

"Even so, RedBrick knows how the campaign scored, right?" I asked.

"Of course, they track everything," he said.

"Does anyone see where we are coming out here?" I asked. Amazingly, nobody seemed to be catching on to what was glaringly apparent to me. How did we get so far removed from thinking like a startup? Maybe it was what I'm doing with Matt that made the problem so clear, but either way, I needed to get this team back on track.

"You've just told me the obvious. We're most likely to lose the RedBrick account if we don't create work that pays off in the real world. However, we have no idea how our work is doing in the marketplace whatsoever. I'm guessing, no actually, I'm quite sure, that RedBrick would share this information with us if we asked. Yet here we are in the dark."

Continuing, I said, "We have to keep it in mind every day that we are partners with RedBrick. We're not working with them to win awards in the trade press or to make sure the CEO likes the company billboard he sees on the way to work. It's always to help them grow their business. That's the first thing we have to reset." I looked around at the group. "Does anyone disagree with this?"

No one answered. I stole a glance at Steve, and he looked a bit beaten down. My purpose for the meeting was not to strip his leadership role, but this was something he fumbled. Ultimately, the success of our relationship with the client was in his hands.

Luckily, Steve was the first to speak. "I'm surprised I missed this. It was my responsibility. We absolutely should be asking—no, demanding—that we have data from RedBrick on how our campaigns are delivering."

He paused for a moment, then continued, "I think we probably became too comfortable with the relationship and lost track of our focus on the results side of the equation. We used to fixate on results."

"You're right on, Steve," I said. "Let's make that one of the first things you and the team work to rediscover."

I then walked them through the analysis I had done on the amount of time they spent in meetings versus actually doing creative work. Just as I had been, they were completely surprised by what it showed. The graph dramatized how their time allotment had shifted too far toward talking and meeting about the work, instead of actually doing the work.

I wanted to push for why we'd gotten to this point, so I asked. "Can anyone tell me how this trend happened? Or why there is such a need for all these meetings?"

Sally, one of the junior team members, spoke up first. "I have to make sure everyone signs off on the work before we send it to the client, and that usually takes multiple meetings."

"Why does everyone need to sign off?" I asked.

"Because that's the process I'm told to follow, I suppose," she said.

I glanced around the room, and my eyes caught Carla's. I said, "Carla, your group creates the strategic plan for the campaign, correct?"

"That's right," she said.

"And that happens at the beginning of the assignment, correct?" I continued, knowing the answer.

"Yep, we set the strategic goal for the campaign at the start, so everyone knows and shares in what we're working toward," she said.

"Great. Sally, in a typical campaign process, how many checkpoints does the strategy team have that require a meeting?" I asked.

"Um…" she said, thinking. "Probably six meetings would be the average."

"Six?!" I said, not believing it. I looked back at Carla and said, "Carla, why would your team need to have so many check-in meetings?"

"Because we need to make sure that throughout the project the team is adhering to our carefully structured strategy," she said, confidently.

"And how often do you find the team is not 'adhering to the strategy,' as you put it?" I asked.

"Well, actually," she paused, thinking, "there very rarely is a discrepancy in what the team is doing and the direction we laid out."

"See!" said Martin, one of our top creatives. "I've been trying to tell you that we don't need so many check-ins. We do read the strategy briefing, you know!"

Carla replied, "It never hurts to double check. It's on me to make sure what we deliver to the client is in line with what we set out to accomplish."

"But Carla," I said, "you just told me that there is almost never an issue with how the team follows the plan. Why do you feel there is a need for so many meetings to double and triple check?"

"I guess..." she said, trying to find the right words. "I guess I just don't trust that, if we're not checking, the team won't refer back to the work my group did."

"Of course we will!" said Martin.

"But in Q4 you didn't, and we ended up having to go back and redesign much of what we had done!" she said, raising her voice to match Martin's.

"And we apologized for that and promised it wouldn't happen again. No one was more affected by that than my team. We had to work an insane amount of hours to get the campaign back on track! At some point you'll have to trust us again," he said.

Trust. Finally, we had gotten to the real point. Before I could weigh in, Steve stood and walked up next to me. He turned to address the team.

"Martin is right, Carla. Your group does have to learn how to trust him again. In fact," he said, looking around at the entire team, "We all have to learn to trust each other more. One of the things I've learned from Will over the years is the importance of how members relate to one another within a team. And I can see clearly now that we've lost the trust we used to have in each other. It's hurting our ability to be the partner to RedBrick that we once were."

He turned and looked at me, and said, "Will, I think I've got this now. If it's all right with you, I'd like to have the team to myself for the rest of our time. We'll work on how to get back on track. By the end of this week, we'll have a plan we all like. Does that sound okay?"

I smiled wide and said, "That sounds great. Good luck you guys. Remember, the more honest you can be while Steve continues this meeting, the better. You'll get to the root of what is causing the trust to break down if you can open up and share your real feelings."

With that, I left the team with Steve and headed back to my desk.

DAY FOUR

It was 9 a.m. on Wednesday morning. The weather was perfect for a walk-and-talk, mid-70's and a bright, clear sky. Matt and I decided to start this meeting—our fourth of the five that we'd be having—walking around the path outside his office. We had just finished a lap and were well into Matt's story about how things had gone Monday morning when everyone realized their office layout had changed.

"Shocked. Yes, I think that's the best description," Matt said. I had asked what the general mood was when each person arrived at the office Monday morning.

"And a kind of child-like amusement as well. Suddenly being in a different environment can be scary and uncomfortable, but also fun in a way. I could see some people enjoying the change. Mostly, they were confused. And then there were the people that lost their offices," he said.

"Right, how did you handle that one?"

"I had an idea on the way into the office that morning about how to handle it. When you've worked your tail off to have an office,

166

you expect that you'll always have it," he said. "So when people came in and saw that their office was gone, and then saw their name on a desk out in the open—a desk that was the same size and setup as everyone else's—they'd come to me with an alarmed look and ask what the deal was. Each time that happened, I countered with, 'Let's talk about it in my office,' and walked them over to my desk. Whey they saw it was the same size and layout as theirs and that I was out in the open also, there was not much they could say." Matt paused. "Well, that is, all but one person."

"Let me guess, our buddy Eric," I said.

"Bingo," he said. "Eric was downright furious. I thought he was on the verge of quitting. He started raising his voice, so I invited him into one of the breakout rooms, where he continued to complain for a solid 30 minutes. Ultimately, I asked if he trusted me to make the right decision. He responded that he wasn't sure anymore! At that point, rather than waiting for him to quit, I was thinking of letting him go. We ultimately decided to cool off and talk again later in the day."

Matt then relayed that throughout the morning, Eric's attitude seemed to worsen. He obviously was annoyed by all the distractions around him. The rest of the team seemed to be adjusting to the new environment. Meetings were happening in the little breakout areas, and the whiteboard wall was coming alive with funny sayings and quotes.

He had let everyone settle in, then gave a talk about why the space had changed so much. He was able to tie everything back to the PVTV (Purpose, Vision, Tenets, and Values) they had adopted together.

"How'd that go, Matt?" I asked.

"I was encouraged by the team's reaction," Matt said. "And by the time I met with Eric later in the day, he had started to come around a little. I decided I'll humor him for the rest of the week and then we'll see."

"And do you think Eric will be in it for the long haul?" I asked.

Matt responded that he thought there was a 50/50 chance. "The good news is that the COO was receptive!"

Matt had done the right thing and met with the COO first thing Monday morning. In fact, Matt had greeted him in the Titan parking lot. By the time they reached Matt's setup, the COO was curious to see the new layout and to hear how this "experiment" was going to play out. As Matt described it to him, the goal was a more efficient and effective team. On Tuesday, Matt met with HR and received approval to make the changes to his team—two team members would need to leave, and he'd have to hire two new pros. I asked if there would be blowback to the changes from current members, and he told me that the team would understand the difference rather than fight against it.

"Okay," I said after Matt was finished catching me up on everything. "Let's recap where we are. You're thinking and acting like an entrepreneur with a *Do or Die Mindset*. Your team is in alignment and working toward a common goal thanks to your newly defined PVTV. Also, you're freshening the team with the right people, in the right positions, with a culture that promotes Trust in the Right People."

"Yep!" Matt smiled proudly. "And all of this in just a little over three weeks!"

"It's good to be past the halfway mark," I broke in. "Now you're ready to master the fourth principle of The Five-Day Turnaround—Move at the Speed of Startup."

"Move at the speed of startup, huh?" Matt sounded curious. "That's kind of what we set out to do in this whole process, isn't it?"

"It's certainly one of the reasons we're doing this. However, our journey is more than that. Reacting quickly to take advantage of business opportunities isn't going to happen if we haven't signed up for the other aspects of thinking like a successful startup. Moving fast requires more than just making quick decisions."

As we made our way around the path, we were coming up on the turn back to his building. "Let's head back to a conference room so I can walk you through Day Four."

"Let me guess. You're going to need a whiteboard again, right?" he said, grinning.

"Busted," I said, laughing.

As we walked through his team's location at Titan, I noticed a palpable difference from what I sensed in my earlier trips there. Usually, on a morning visit, a significant number of his team members had yet to arrive. But now the place was bustling with energy and motion from a full complement of team members. It was a startling transformation from what I had experienced just a week ago.

I shared my impression with Matt as he closed the door to the conference room.

"I know, it's quite remarkable how much more people communicate already."

"I'm curious to know how many times you've had meetings in a breakout room instead of just talking at your desk out in the open?" I inquired.

He looked toward the ceiling for a moment while he thought. "Not many, actually. I thought that would be a big issue, but I've had most of my conversations right there at my desk. We talk a little more quietly than before because we don't want to disturb others. What I'm finding is that most of my conversations are not very sensitive in nature. You were right about that."

"Good. There will be times that you'll need a room, but I find it isn't nearly as often as even I expected when I first made the switch. Okay, let's get rolling."

I walked up to the whiteboard and wrote at the top: Move at the Speed of Startup. Underneath it, I put four bullet points for carrying it out. When I finished, the fourth startup trait looked like this:

Move at the Speed of Startup

- **Focus, focus, focus**
- **Lead by example**
- **Embrace the MVP**
- **Remove speed bumps**

"Let's start by talking about focus. That's the first step in unlocking your ability to move fast. Let's look at where you're focusing your time and energy on a daily, weekly, and monthly basis."

"We start by focusing on the one thing that needs to be accomplished today—this day, not any other." I continued. "Each new day you need to know what matters most to get done by you personally. Do you ever do that, start the day by making sure you know what you must accomplish by bedtime?"

"Not really. I guess some days I do, like on Monday it was easy to know that the most important thing was pulling off the changes to our office space. But on a day-to-day basis, I can't say that I make a point to focus in that way," he said.

"Most people don't. The problem is that if you aren't sure where to focus your time, the day will dictate it for you," I said.

I added a line to the whiteboard:

Move at the Speed of Startup

- **Focus, focus, focus**
  - o **Daily: One Thing**
- **Lead by example**
- **Embrace the MVP**
- **Remove speed bumps**

"So, each day I want you to start by writing down the one thing that you are going to focus on that day. Have you read the book *The One Thing*, by Gary Keller?" I asked.

"No, I haven't, but I'm guessing I need to?"

"Yes, it's your homework assignment. I brought you a copy," I said, pulling out the book and handing it to him. "But even before you dive into the book, you can start each day as I described by getting your head around the one thing you need to accomplish that day."

"Roger," he said.

"Now, let's compare our calendars," I said, pulling out my laptop. I had asked Matt to bring his laptop to this meeting, so he fired his up as well.

Sitting next to each other, we compared our calendars side-by-side.

"Wow, the two of them don't look like they're in the same universe as each other," he said, laughing.

I agreed, "No, they don't. What strikes you as most different?"

"Well, first of all, my calendar is so much more crowded than yours! I guess that comes with working at a larger company."

"I'm not sure that's it. Hold on a second," I said. I changed the date on my calendar to look at a week three years in the past. It looked exactly like Matt's.

"This is what my calendar looked like not so long ago," I said.

"Huh. That looks a lot more like mine. Your company was even smaller back then. What happened?"

"Well, I realized I needed openings in my calendar to be flexible, to react to what the day or week brought. I also needed a little time just to think. Both of those things were impossible when my calendar was booked completely. So, I started focusing on leaving nice-sized gaps in my schedule. It was difficult at first because I had to say 'no' to a bunch of things or push them into the following weeks. But once I got into that groove, it became much easier."

"But I have so much that demands my attention. All those things I need to approve or actually handle." Matt shook his head. "I don't see how I can add a bunch of free time into my schedule."

"Ah, there's the other thing," I responded. "I started delegating more. Actually, delegating a ton of stuff. It was hard at first, but you learn quickly that your team members can handle much more than you think. And giving them more responsibility is the best thing you can do for them. It shows your trust and belief in them, and it shows them what they can accomplish."

I walked up to the board and added:

Move at the Speed of Startup

- **Focus, focus, focus**
  - o **Daily: One Thing**
  - o **Weekly: Manage your calendar**
- **Lead by example**
- **Embrace the MVP**
- **Remove speed bumps**

He was writing in his notebook and said, "Okay, I can definitely do a better job at delegating. All comes back to trust, doesn't it?"

Not waiting for me to reply, he continued, "So, I get it. Each day decide what I need to focus on, and each week, I'm guessing Monday morning, look at my calendar and make sure there's enough time to think and also react to the week's events. Is that right?"

"That's right. Do you notice anything else that's different about my calendar?"

"Yes, it looks like someone spilled a box of Skittles all over it! I've never seen so much color on someone's calendar before."

"It does look pretty, doesn't it?" I laughed. "I don't use color for the visual aesthetics. I do it to understand what I'm spending time on. When I glance at my calendar, I can see how much time that week was for Work, Family, Doing Good, and what I call "Random." Each activity has a color associated with it, and whenever something goes on my calendar, it gets the appropriate color."

"So this week," he said, looking at my calendar, "you have many green colored events. What does that signify?"

"Green is Work, and, yes, I do have a lot of work events on my calendar this week. If I look at any week, and I have too much Yellow, which represents Random, or too little Pink, which represents Doing Good, I try to make the appropriate changes to stay balanced."

"I see how it works," Matt said. "Although in my case the entire calendar would be green. My goal should be to identify my areas of focus and then color-code accordingly."

"Excellent. So if you do those two things—make sure you're not too busy during the week and color-code your entries—you'll be on the right track. The third and final step in this category is a monthly check-up."

I walked up to the whiteboard and added the word "Headspace."

Move at the Speed of Startup

- **Focus, focus, focus**
  - o **Daily: One Thing**
  - o **Weekly: Manage your calendar**
  - o **Monthly: Headspace**
- **Lead by example**
- **Embrace the MVP**
- **Remove speed bumps**

"Headspace? What's that?" Matt asked.

"Headspace is what I call the big things that I should be keeping in mind. It's usually less than five things, and more like one or two. See, each day you have little things that you need to be accomplishing, and weekly you need to make sure you're spending your time in the right ways, but if you only do that much, you'll forget to make progress on your big goals.

"See, as the leader," I continued, "you have to make sure the team is focused and aligned on a day-to-day basis, and you also have to make sure the team is accomplishing its bigger mission. To do both, I have what I call 'Headspace.'"

"Can I ask what your Headspace focus areas are right now?" he asked.

"Sure," I said. "As you know, I use Evernote to keep track of all my notes. There's a tag in Evernote called #headspace. Right now I have three Headspace focus areas—#5dayturnaround, #RedBrick, and #Vision2020. The first is what we're doing, the second is a big client initiative, and the third is a vision-mapping exercise to help me see where we want to be by 2020, which I'll share with the staff."

"And I notice under each of those you have a bunch of notes?"

"As I have thoughts that apply to any of these challenges, I put a plug in Evernote with the tag #headspace, and then I can easily find the reference when I work on that initiative."

"And how often do you review your Headspace initiatives?" he asked.

"I try to look at it daily and see if there are things I need to do, but it's more of a 'several times a week' thing. And then I try to commit time in my calendar to deal with the Headspace initiatives. Often I'll make myself get out of the office for a few hours to get away from the distractions and make progress carrying out my Headspace focus."

He was writing notes furiously, and I could tell this was something he would be trying. Once Matt was done, I moved on to the next point.

"Now that you know the steps required to handle your time better, let's look at 'Lead by Example.' If you want your team to begin moving fast, they'll have to see you moving fast. You can't be a bottleneck in decision-making. You need to fight the urge to descend into 'analysis paralysis.'

"About being a bottleneck, is that a problem currently?" I asked.

"Well, it definitely can be at times, but after our talk about delegating more, I see one way to deal with it. I'm going to start pushing things down the line, letting my team members make the decision more often. That should reduce the number of times I end up as a bottleneck or slow things down."

"Great! So look for ways to show your team it's okay to make decisions quickly, and that a speedy decision is always better than no decision.

"The final thing here is that to grow the company fast, you need to make sure that you and your team are open to experimenting with new ideas. Playing it safe has no place in a successful startup's mindset. For the past 20 years, my mentor Charles has been compiling a list of what he calls 'Idea Killers' that restrict innovative thinking. They're expressions like, 'It doesn't grab me,' or 'Bring that up again next month,' or 'Great idea but not for us.' He put all these hurdles together in a 99 Idea Killers poster with the graphic of a fierce dragon shouting, 'Beware! They can eat you alive!'"

I pulled one of the posters out of my bag and handed it to Matt. "Be sure to convey to the team that no idea is born perfect. Progress means championing new ideas and giving them a chance to grow."

"Wow. He's got 99 ways to say 'No' here, and I've heard most of them at Titan. I'm going to put the poster up where everyone can see it. The more our team is open to blazing new trails, the faster we'll move and the more effective we'll be."

"Exactly. I'll tell Charles you're a fan," I said with a wink.

I stood back up and walked to the whiteboard. "The next one is a big one. Are you aware of the MVP, the Minimum Viable Product?"

"Can't say that I am."

"It's common in the startup world, but most established companies haven't heard of it. MVP flips the process of building a product on its head. Instead of spending an endless amount of time planning and perfecting every aspect of a product or service, and then launching it, the MVP model says to flush out the very minimum of an idea and get it into the user's hands as fast as possible. It's a great way to learn quickly what the user wants, likes, and dislikes so you can do the work to perfect the offering quickly. It increases your speed to market and improves your ability to produce exactly what the customer wants, rather than working so hard on what you imagine they will want," I explained.

He was nodding. "Okay, yep, I get this one. I can think of several things we're doing right now that I bet would turn out better following the MVP model. It would help us cut to the chase rapidly, and use our time more efficiently."

"Exactly," I said, glad he was getting it. "Now, let's look at the last action listed under the Move at the Speed of Startup traits. The one headlined, 'Remove Speed Bumps.' Any clue what this one is about?"

"Sounds obvious enough. A speed bump slows someone down, so I need to look for anything that is slowing my team down, and remove it."

"Right. Think for a minute. What might be slowing your team down?" I asked.

He took a deep breath and thought for a minute, then said, "Certainly me being a bottleneck, but we talked about that. I'm guessing we have certain processes set up that slow the team down. I can make a note to review that. Also, we have too many required meetings that are stopping us from moving quickly."

"That's even something we're battling. Meetings can be huge speed bumps. Did you ever create that list of your peers and your relationship with them?" I asked.

"Yep, have it right here," he said, flipping his notebook back a few pages.

Matt showed me a list of the seven people at Titan who were his peers. He included the CEO. He had grades next to each one. There were several A's and B's and a couple of C's.

"Interesting, so the grades represent the strength of your relationship with the individual, correct?" I asked.

"Right. Instead of numbers, I thought grades would help me better see where I stood with different people. There are a few men and women that I have what I'd call an 'A relationship' with— like our COO. I've spent time with them and we have mutual trust, which is probably why he was cool with me changing the marketing team's office layout. And some B's, like the HR leader and my CEO. Also a couple of C's, mainly because I haven't spent much time with them to strengthen the relationship," he said.

"Got it. So, why do you think I wanted you to get into this one?"

"I think I get it. There are times when the support of my peers will be critical to Move with the Speed of Startup. If they're not on board, it could slow my team down."

"Exactly! Anything you want to achieve that will take a major change will need support from some of your peers. I hesitate to call it internal politics, but that's kind of what it is. You've always been strong at building relationships, so I had guessed that this would be easy for you. It's hugely important, and something I want you to watch."

"Makes sense. I love the metaphor of removing speed bumps. Really, all of the things we talked about today are parts of what needs to happen. I feel like I can start acting on the entire list immediately."

I smiled, certain that if I had met with Matt four weeks ago and walked him through these concepts and behaviors, he would have laughed me out of the building. Now, not only was Matt embracing the work, he was excited about what might be possible.

"That's great, Matt!" I said. "There are two assignments to work on before our last meeting—besides starting to read the book I gave you. The first is to check out where you're focusing your time. The second is to ask yourself and your team, each time a project comes up, 'can we get this done faster and remain just as effective?' Is there an MVP model that could be applied here?' Make sense to you?"

He nodded and said, "Makes perfectly good sense."

We made some small talk, and I headed out, realizing more than ever that my own agency could use some of this advice.

Back at my company on Monday afternoon, the first order of business was to talk with Steve about the plan he and his team had come up with for RedBrick.

He was waiting for me when I got in. "Boss, you ready?" He had a look on his face that I hadn't seen in a while. Was it excitement?

"You bet, let's do it," I said, and followed Steve to a small conference room he'd reserved for our talk. I sat down at the table, and Steve closed the door. He dropped a document in front of me that read "RedBrick Advertising Agency RFP" in bold letters.

"What's this?" I asked, confused. The idea that RedBrick had asked for an RFP from the agency to hold onto their business was shocking. Clearly, their CMO hadn't been honest with me about the state of our relationship if the account was up for review.

These thoughts were flying through my mind. Steve noticed and brought me back to reality. "Whoa there, Will, I can see the panic in your face! I didn't mean to scare you. This is not an official RFP process from RedBrick. We created this RFP to help us reshape how we are delivering for them."

I unclenched my jaw and my fists and breathed a sigh of relief. "Steve, you almost gave me a heart attack! Next time, warn me before you put something like this in front of me."

Laughing, he said, "Will do."

"Okay, so tell me about this RFP you've created."

"After you left our meeting the other day, we started listing all the things we've been doing out of fear and distrust. We soon realized that we had fallen into many of the same bad traits that frustrated us about RedBrick! Lots of unnecessary meetings, too many approvals, playing it too safe. We decided to rethink the entire relationship. What if we had to repitch the account? What would we do differently? How would we structure the partnership? That got us thinking, why not create a virtual RFP that included the expectations from both sides—the agency and the client—and then work against that to rethink what is needed. So, that's just what we did," he said, sounding proud.

"That's a great approach! It's easy to get stale and less creative over time. Going through an RFP process delivers a fresh look at the prospect's situation and totally new solutions to their problems. I love it, well done!" I said, thrilled by their original approach.

"Glad you like it," he said. He was obviously pleased. I sensed his passion.

Steve walked me through the RFP. The team had identified many vital interactions. A few stood out for me as critical areas.

First, there was a section in the front that had been written by the "client." Of course, it was our team writing on behalf of RedBrick. It laid out how RedBrick would be a client partner that was quick to respond to agency requests for information and, more importantly, that would commit to being forthcoming with an honest appraisal of agency performance. It stated that every Friday morning, Steve and the CMO would touch base by phone to share a clear-eyed look at what was happening in the relationship.

"That call might be five minutes, or it might be an hour, depending on what's going on at the time. The point is to have a set weekly no-holds-barred exchange with each other," he explained.

The document then laid out several things that RedBrick would want in their agency relationship. There was a specific section called "Time Allocation" that stated that at no point should there be more than 10% of agency time spent in meetings and at no point should creative work take up less than 40% of billable time.

As he walked me through that section, he said, "These are actually guiding principles for our team. We believe that if we have clear rules for how we want to operate, we'll be better at sticking to them. Otherwise, we might fall into the same old bad habits."

I liked the idea but needed to know if it was possible. "How are you going to keep meetings to 10% or less of time devoted to RedBrick? That's a huge difference compared to how your team currently operates," I said.

"It won't be easy, but we have a few ideas. One is that we have 'standing meetings,' which means no more chairs. In fact, we already took the chairs out of the conference room we use. The thinking there is that if we all have to stand, meetings will be shorter. I think you shared that stunt with me at one point," he said.

I nodded. This was good thinking. Steve had momentum. He continued to share ways the team would replace pointless meetings with more time pursuing meaningful creative breakthroughs.

He walked me through the rest of the deck and said that he planned to take the RedBrick CMO through the make-believe RFP and then present the new thinking to both teams in three weeks. There would be a fresh strategic direction, new creative executions, and, of course, a better way to monitor the relationship.

When he finished, I said, "Steve, this is excellent work! I couldn't be happier with the way you and the team came together and got to the heart of the situation. My only question is, how did we get into this position in the first place?"

"That's easy, Will," he said, without needing any time to consider the question. "Fear. We were afraid that we might lose the business if we took a risk and failed. Over time, we became complacent to producing 'okay' results, as long as we weren't taking any risky chances."

He chuckled and shook his head. "We became a perfect case study from that book you had our leadership team read, *The Innovator's Dilemma.*

"I couldn't have put it better myself," I smiled. "Keep me posted on how Mark reacts." We headed out of the conference room.

Charles and I had agreed to meet on Saturday morning for a bike ride. It was his suggestion, of course.

"Hey, Charles, where do you want to stop?" I was struggling to catch my breath but trying not to show it. I realized just how out of shape I was. Charles was decades older than me, and he was kicking my butt.

"Soon! There's a great place just five miles up," he said, not quite getting it that "five miles" wasn't "soon" to me. I didn't have much choice except to continue to struggle along behind him. Finally, we pulled into the rest area, hopped off our bikes, grabbed our water bottles, and walked to a bench that overlooked a massive park. The view was spectacular.

"Not bad, is it?" Charles asked, pointing to the expanse below us.

"Stunning. I need to get up here more often."

"If not for cycling, I doubt I ever would have found this gem," Charles said.

I was feeling better about the ride. "You know, that reminds me. I have to tell you about the breakthrough we had at the agency this week," I said, and shared the plan that Steve had come up with for RedBrick.

Charles was impressed. "Remarkable! That should become standard practice for you at the agency."

"I was thinking the same thing. If this goes well with RedBrick, I think we'll institute it for all of our clients. I'm thinking after two years of the relationship, we respond to a virtual RFP of our own making."

"Imagine if you told a potential new client that every two years, you'd be doing the equivalent of repitching the business. It could be a great addition to your sales process and the best way to keep them from ever putting the account up for bid," he said.

Then the conversation shifted to Titan, which was the main reason I wanted to meet with him. I briefed him on the week's events, sharing the progress that Matt had made with his team, including the complete overhaul of the office layout. Charles was impressed by how readily Matt was making changes.

"It sounds like you inspired Matt at just the right time," he said. "The fact that he jumped into this transformation so quickly tells me he might have left Titan if not for this process."

"You could be right. He seems like a completely different person. He's more relaxed, and he seems more positive about the team. The only thing I'm worried about is that he hasn't had to deal with failing at any of this as of yet."

"Ah. Is that the final stage of your turnaround process?" he asked.

"That's right. The successful startup trait for the Day Five meeting is Welcome Failure."

"That's bound to be difficult for him," Charles said. "It sounds like you've set things up to give him the best chance to embrace it. A team needs to know that it's okay to take chances, as long as you're learning from the mistakes."

We continued discussing how successful startups deal with failure. Charles shared stories about how he successfully built a Welcome Failure mentality at his past companies. It all came down to how willing the leader was to be vulnerable. If he or she is afraid to put themselves out there and risk failing in front of their peers and team members, they can't create a culture that welcomes failure.

As we walked back to our bikes, Charles said, "So, one more session, and then The Five-Day Turnaround is complete. Are you still up to meet next Friday?"

"Yep, I have us down for 8 a.m. at The Steaming Cup."

"Great. Can you do me a favor, Will? Over this next week, think about what you've learned through this process. I know you're helping Matt make big changes, but I'm gathering that you're learning just as much, perhaps more. I'd like to hear your reflections on that when we meet," he said.

"Absolutely," I said. Even the positive changes with the RedBrick account were due to this process I was taking Matt through.

We hopped on our bikes and took off back down the hill. I was smiling wide, not just because we were going downhill (though that was a welcome change). In truth, I was feeling good because I knew deep down that we were on to something significant with The Five-Day Turnaround.

I was eager to take Matt through the final step of the process.

DAY FIVE

Pulling into the parking lot at Titan for the Day Five meeting, it felt like an entire year had gone by in the four weeks since the journey with Matt began. I'd become a welcome figure at Titan, particularly for Matt's team. I was rooting for them to be successful. I was going to miss these frequent visits.

I high-fived Mrs. Kay as I passed her in the lobby heading for Matt's desk. I found him there, typing away on his laptop, and I took a moment to take in the scene. There was Matt, sitting right out in the open with nothing to signify that he was the boss. He was clearly a member of the team.

He noticed me and said, "Oh, hey, didn't see you there. Just finishing up a few things, let's meet in our usual conference room."

"Sounds good. See you in there," I said. As I set up in the conference room, I recapped on the whiteboard the traits we had worked on so far.

The Goal: To Act More Like A Successful Startup

1. **The Do or Die Mindset**
2. **Live Your PVTV (Purpose, Vision, Tenets, and Values)**
3. **Trust in the Right People**
4. **Move at the Speed of Startup**
5.

Just as I finished number four, Matt walked in and took a seat. He looked up at the whiteboard and said, "We certainly have accomplished quite a bit, haven't we?"

"I was just thinking the same thing. Let's start today with you walking me through the first steps to acting more like a startup," I said.

"A successful startup," he corrected, smiling.

"Yes, right, good catch."

"Okay, so let me give this a try. To act more like a successful startup, a leader at an established, slow-moving company must first embrace the Do or Die Mindset, which essentially means thinking like the CEO of a startup. To do this, the leader must have..." he grabbed his notebook and flipped back a few pages,

"...an unflinching belief in her or his self, fearlessness, and be results-oriented."

I nodded, suggesting he should continue.

"And once leaders are in the right mindset, they must define and live the PVTV for their team. That's their shared Purpose, Vision, Tenets, and Values. PVTV helps everyone focus on the important things and travel in the same direction."

"Perfect," I said.

"And once the team has their PVTV defined and operationalized, the leader must make sure to Trust in the Right People. You have a well-constructed team of people, organized against your goals that fit with your Values and are in the right position to be effective."

He looked to me for reassurance, and I indicated that he was getting it right.

Matt continued, "And when the leader has the right mindset, the team is aligned, and the right people are in the right environment to be successful, the group is ready to start Moving at the Speed of Startup. To do this, the leader must stay focused and manage work time well. The team should embrace the MVP concept, and not let speed bumps slow them down."

He said this last part without referring to his notes, so I knew it was starting to sink in.

"Great! And how has Move at the Speed of Startup been going so far? I know it's only been a few days, but you had a few homework assignments if I remember correctly."

Matt walked me through how he had reorganized his calendar, and proudly showed me the color scheme he had created to signify different types of meetings and time allocation. He also shared how he was making sure to have a "one thing" daily focus, and how he was going to keep track of his Headspace priorities.

"The biggest change so far, however," he said, "was asking the team what we can move along faster, and if there was an MVP model we could apply. I held a town hall meeting out in the middle of the team's space to explain what an MVP was and then tasked each member to answer the two key questions. I also decided to put a bounty on who came to me by the end of the day with the most ideas."

"What was the prize?" I asked.

"A lunch with me and the CEO, which I cleared with him beforehand of course," he said.

"And did it work?"

"Boy did it ever!" he said. "I got almost 50 ideas from across the team. I was blown away. Even more exciting is that we implemented some of the ideas immediately! There is no doubt that we're already starting to move faster just by going through that one exercise."

"That's terrific! Great idea to offer the prize."

I stood up and said, "Okay, the final piece of the Five-Day Turnaround might be the toughest. It's around the concept of failing."

He looked at me and nodded his head. "Right, I can see how, with all the steps we've taken so far, we're going to have some initiatives fail down the road."

Once again, two steps forward, one step back.

"Actually, Matt," I said, "You should be failing more. The challenge is to flip how you think about failing."

I walked up to the whiteboard and added: 5. Welcome Failure.

"What? Will, I'm sorry, but this one doesn't make any sense to me. Why would I welcome failure? You've talked about us working as a team, but what team likes to fail?" He was visibly bothered by the idea.

"As I said, you have to change how you respond to whatever the word "failure" connotes. I'm not talking about failing to hit your goals, not at all. I'm talking about a purposeful process of using failure to get to your goals.

"See," I continued, "you want people to take chances. If team members are afraid to fail, they will focus on avoiding it, which will make them cautious and less willing to think outside the box. You need to help them push their fear of failure aside. Ultimately, you'll all benefit from the lessons that failure teaches you. Many of the startups that succeed over the long run have a history of stumbling along the way, especially dealing with false starts in their early years."

I could see he still wasn't getting it, so I decided to jump into the first action step of the Welcome Failure trait.

On the right side of the board, I wrote:

Welcome Failure

1. Fail Fast

"You want to fail fast. Taking forever to have a shortfall is a sure sign that you are not attempting anything truly extraordinary. You have to push to test your new ideas sooner rather than later. To fail fast is to learn fast," I said.

"I can see that. Kind of like the MVP model?" Matt asked.

"Exactly! The MVP can lead to failing fast at some aspect of what you have in mind. It also can get you to the overall goal with blazing speed. If the experiment you try isn't working, you can shut it down and move onto the next possibility quickly. This bold approach led people to conquer space and make some of the most trailblazing medical cures come to life."

I added the next instruction to the list.

Welcome Failure

1. Fail Fast
2. Fail Often

"Oh, I gotta hear what you mean by this." Matt was chuckling.

Laughing, I fired back, "I know it sounds crazy, but trust me, it works better than hardly ever failing at a task. The goal is to make sure your team constantly tries new things. If you aren't failing enough, then you aren't trying enough. Have you ever heard Thomas Edison's comment about his failures when creating the light bulb?"

"No, can't say that I have."

"He said that he failed 1,000 times before he was able to come up with the answer. Only he didn't explain it quite that way. He said that creating the light bulb took 1,000 steps. He knew that without those failures, he never would have invented the light bulb."

"That makes sense, but we're not inventing anything in the Marketing Department," he said.

"Growth Department," I said, correcting him. "True, but you are trying to invent a better outcome for your customers. So you need your team to have the confidence to test multiple alternatives in the search for a winner. I'd bet a good number of those tests could fail, wouldn't you agree?"

"I can't argue with that. Okay, is the next one 'fail always'?" he asked with a laugh.

"No, not quite, we don't want to always fail," I said. "In fact, we only want to make new mistakes."

I added that next truth to the whiteboard:

Welcome Failure

1. **Fail Fast**
2. **Fail Often**
3. **Only Make New Mistakes**

"What do you think that means?" I asked.

"Well, that's pretty self-explanatory, I think. It means that we'll make mistakes along the way, but the goal is to learn from them and not repeat any," he said.

"Perfect. This is a mantra you want to share with your team. They need to know that it's okay to make mistakes, but it's not okay to make the same mistake twice. If they do, it means they didn't learn anything from the experience of failure."

He wrote that down and said, "Love it. I think I'll teach my kids that one as well."

Good for him, I thought. I added the last element to the whiteboard.

Welcome Failure

1. **Fail Fast**
2. **Fail Often**
3. **Only Make New Mistakes**
4. **Reward Failure**

"The final element in showing that you Welcome Failure is to Reward Failure willingly. You have to create an environment where the staff is unafraid to fail. Part of doing this is to reward failure—especially outstanding failure."

"Outstanding failure? Dude, you're killing me here," he said. "What do you consider an outstanding failure?"

"I would say an outstanding failure is an experiment that goes beyond anything ever seen before and that failed in a big way—but the failure did not stop the team from losing faith or from ultimately reaching the goal. By rewarding extreme failures, you show your team that you want their best ideas, not just their 'safe' ideas," I said.

"Hmmm..." Matt nodded slowly. He was starting to get it.

I needed to give him a personal example to drive home the point. Luckily, I had the perfect one. "Let me tell you about a time my agency took a chance on a pitch to a new client. We were pitching for something we really had no business going after, so we knew we had to take some chances. We knew that if it didn't pay off, no harm was done because the odds were stacked against us to win anyway.

"Our big creative idea for the account was around 'surprise and delight,' so our Creative Director suggested that we try to bring that to life in the pitch. We hired a professional opera singer to be on standby outside of the conference room. After we unveiled the creative idea to the client, suddenly there was a booming voice coming from outside the door singing the national anthem. The door opened and in came the opera singer, who continued to sing as loudly as she could, belting out a beautiful rendition of the national anthem. The client was surprised and shaken, and not remotely impressed."

"I think I would have had the same reaction," Matt said.

"Likely, yes. After the meeting, I asked the CMO of the prospect how that came off, and he said, 'Let's just say it didn't help you at all.' I appreciated his honesty. Clearly, we didn't win the business, and we never tried anything as far out as that one again. Still, it was worth a try."

"I get it, and you would never have taken that chance in a pitch where you had a real shot. So, you gave yourself the ability to get creative and learn something. You took a chance on a long shot and missed, but you were better for it."

"Yep," I agreed. "Even an outstanding failure can be welcome. Maybe the next time out there'll be an outstanding success."

It was time to wrap it up, so I looked at Matt and said, "The next step is for you to share a failure with the team. They need to see that you're willing to admit to making mistakes. You have to show them it's okay to try and to fail. Only then will they feel like it's an acceptable thing for them to do."

"Uh...what if I can't think of anything to share?" he asked, sheepishly.

I laughed and said, "Oh, I'm sure between the two of us, we can think of some ways you failed while we were at Crackersnap."

"Ah, yes, well I can definitely think of a few times I messed up back then. Okay, I'll give it a shot," he said.

"I knew you'd come around," I said with a wink. "So now your homework is to talk to your team about failure, share a time when you failed in an outstanding fashion, and you'll probably want to think about the best way to bring this all to life for them. Perhaps it's another competition. Just find some way to celebrate failure that makes sense for your team. Oh, and make it clear that you're also going to set up new ways to celebrate success!"

"Got it," he said, writing in his notebook. "So that's it?"

"Well, there is one more thing. Let's plan for a catch-up call on Friday morning, and, after you update me on the week's events, you can tell me if you're ready to choose us as your agency. Beware, you should only do that if you still want to work with me after I spent this past month putting you through the process of figuring out how your team can function like an agile startup." I paused, serious. "Really, Matt, if you still don't think you can pull off what we proposed, it is okay if we're not the agency for you."

Matt was quiet for a moment, considering. "Ah, right. I guess technically, if we're going to work with you all on the campaign, we'd need to start next Monday. I've really got some things to think about this week. Talk to you on Friday morning," he said.

Before leaving, I took a photo with my phone of the final whiteboard breakdown and texted it to Charles.

The Goal: To Act More Like A Successful Startup

1. **The Do or Die Mindset**
2. **Live your PVTV (Purpose, Vision, Tenets, and Values)**
3. **Trust in the Right People**
4. **Move at the Speed of Startup**
5. **Welcome Failure**

I woke up the next morning feeling like I hadn't slept at all. I tossed and turned all night, more than once catching an elbow and a "Keep quiet over there!" from Sarah.

I was stressed about how Matt was handling everything and whether he would choose our agency. Plus, the big RedBrick "RePitch Extravaganza," as my team was calling it, was happening tomorrow. This week would shape the direction for our agency for years to come.

As I was dragging myself out of bed, my phone pinged. The sound indicated I had a message from someone on my Priority Contact list. It was an email from Matt.

Will,

It turns out, failing is fun :)

After our time together yesterday, I called a town hall meeting and shared one of the mistakes that I made at Crackersnap. I'm not going to lie, it was embarrassing, but it was also freeing! I made sure to tie the failure back to the lessons that I learned from missing the mark, and how the entire effort ended up being a win.

Then the coolest thing happened. Several other people jumped in and shared similar failure stories. I told everyone that I wanted them to take chances, and emphasized that we want to make only NEW mistakes.

To bring it home, I created a contest where we would all vote at the end of the quarter on who had the best example of welcoming failure. The team is pretty charged up about what I have asked them to do. For now, I will sign off on any experimentation someone wants to try. I hope that's okay. The team suggested we call it "The Quarterly Titanic Failure."

One more thing. Late in the afternoon, we had a pre-planned brainstorming meeting with a few other departments. At the end of the session we had 22 ideas, and the person running the meeting had each person indicate which one they thought had the best chance of working. He was going to pick the idea that got the most votes.

When it was Eric's turn to vote, he stood up and informed everyone that our team liked the MVP approach that could lead to failing fast and often.

He suggested that we should pick a variety of ideas and run tests against all of them, instead of choosing the one we all like the most. His point of view was a huge hit, and that's exactly what ended up happening!

Thanks,
Matt

I replied:

AMAZING! And, yes, I think having you approve the experiments at this point is smart.

Eric sounds like he's become the biggest fan of the turnaround. Who would have thought!

Best,
Will

It was still early in the process, but I couldn't have asked for better progress. And creating a competition for the best/worst failure was a truly daring move.

I finished getting ready for the day with a pep in my step and made my way to the office.

As I settled in at my desk, I received two texts within minutes of each other. They will go down as two of the best client messages I've ever received.

The first was from Mark, the CMO of RedBrick. It read:

> *Will, your team just blew us away. Absolutely BLEW US AWAY. Couldn't be happier about our renewed partnership. Just wanted you to know.*

Before I could even reply to that one, I received a text from Matt:

> *I know you love to fail, but this time you didn't. We're in. Send over the paperwork. And why not make it an Agency of Record contract?*

I sat back in my chair, smiled, and breathed a huge, glorious sigh of relief.

The Steaming Cup was busier than usual on this Friday morning. Luckily, I was able to find a table for two and settled down with my laptop to get some work done before Charles showed up. I made my way through my Morning Ritual, knocking out emails and going over my calendar.

I caught Charles' eye as he entered the cafe. He pointed at the register and mouthed, "want anything?" and I shook my head no, lifting my mug to let him know I was set. Five minutes later he arrived at my table with his coffee.

"Well, I gotta know—what ended up happening? How did Matt take in the Welcome Failure startup trait? Any news on winning the business? What about RedBrick—any good news there?" he asked.

I smiled a big grin and updated him on how well everything was going. He responded that he was happy for me, but not surprised. Charles was always a bigger believer in me than I was in myself.

"The key with Matt and his team will be keeping tabs on their progress while keeping in mind that you now have a new agency-client relationship. You'll both have to be careful not to fall back into bad habits."

"You're right," I agreed. "I'll need to find a consistent way to keep track of how the turnaround is holding up." I made an entry in my Evernote.

"You know, it's surprising how far the process you created for thinking like a startup has come. I remember when you first asked me about it," he said.

"The process that *we* created." I corrected him. "Don't discount how much you helped me along the way, Charles! I absolutely could not have done this without your support and wisdom."

"Well, I appreciate that. But you did all the hard work. I just got to weigh in here and there. So," he continued, "where does this leave you? Do you think you might be looking at ways to adapt The Five-Day Turnaround for other clients or other teams within your company?"

"Oh, you know me," I smiled and nodded. "I have some thoughts along those lines. What do you think of the book title, *The 5-Day Turnaround?*"

EPILOGUE

As the Lyft rounded the corner, I could see the conference venue. It was only three months ago that my book, *The 5-Day Turnaround*, hit the shelves. Already, I had done a good amount of speaking at some exciting business conferences. It was hard to believe that it had been 18 months since I first started the turnaround journey with Matt, or that my goal at that point was to use the approach to win his account.

It had, and then so much more had happened too. For one, the process of applying the outstanding traits of successful startups at slow-moving companies has shaped much of what our agency offers.

Soon after I finished the five-day process with Matt at Titan, the CMO of RedBrick heard about what we'd done. He asked me to lunch to learn more. That conversation led us to design a workshop for him that adapted the Titan model to overcome weak links in how RedBrick marketing operated. That offering went well, so we decided to make it a standard offering from our agency. We'd found that in the whirlwind digital economy, many established companies are challenged to figure out how to become more like a startup that performs at breakneck speed.

This approach has become a big selling point for the agency. Management is attracted to us because they know we can help them keep pace with the disruptive startups in their space.

Titan marketing continues to excel. Already, our team has won several advertising awards for groundbreaking work we are doing with them. Matt startled his competitors by taking the kind of chances you would expect from a successful startup, not a legacy corporation.

The Lyft dropped me off, and I made my way into the conference center. I was one of the first conference participants to arrive. I'd be the first speaker of the day. I got busy checking out the room and becoming comfortable with the surroundings. It was a big space with giant TV screens on each side of the podium. Word was that there would be 1,500 people in attendance. It would be the largest audience I had ever addressed.

I made my way up to the stage and walked around, looking out at the empty ballroom and imagining what it would look like when all the people arrived. I went over the first lines of my talk. The opening was always carefully memorized. I pictured myself going through the rest of the presentation.

As I hopped down from the stage, my phone pinged. It was a text from Matt.

> *Good luck up there today. Wish I could be there, but I made sure that Eric would be in attendance. Always good when the CGO of your favorite client is in the audience. ;)*

Six months ago, after his CEO decided to retire, the Board of Titan had promoted Matt to CEO, based mainly on the success he had over the previous year. He promptly promoted Eric to Chief Growth Officer.

I smiled, shot back a thumbs-up emoji, and went out to mingle with the early arrivers. This was going to be a good day.

The journey continues.

Appendix

WORKBOOK

INTRODUCTION

Welcome to *The 5-Day Turnaround* Workbook. The personal reflections and activities provided here are created to help you shape your thoughts, goals, and approaches as you embrace a journey like the one Matt took to move his team to act more like a successful startup.

Each section in the workbook offers an opportunity for self-reflection and a series of activities to help guide your team through The Five-Day Turnaround plan. To reach the full benefit of this workbook, designate a block of time—at the same time—each week for five weeks. The discipline will help you work through the reflections and activities in a process-driven manner that will help you see progress as you work through the exercises.

Begin each section by writing your answer to the Personal Reflection prompt. As you engage the Teamwork exercises, that thinking should offer a framework for processing the conversations and feedback that arise as you work with your department or team.

Our sincere hope is that, as you complete your own Five-Day Turnaround process, you will have had the opportunity to create more confidence, support, and quick wins for yourself as a leader and for your team (or organization)!

DAY ONE

The Do or Die Mindset

The Do or Die Mindset is how you present yourself to your organization and the marketplace. Possessing an unflinching belief in yourself as a leader, leading with fearlessness and tying all your work to results are the pillars of the Do or Die Mindset. Below are reflections and activities to get you started.

Personal Reflection

What is the current state of your department?

What are the hurdles to overcome? List specifics that are creating the hurdles. Think about the impact of issues like confidence, targeted quick wins, and internal support and politics. Where is your department or team stuck? List specific examples. Where are processes or decisions slowed by an overabundance of caution?

Teamwork
Part One: Implementing the Do or Die Mindset

Your Environment:

Is your physical environment impeding productivity? What opportunities exist to think through your existing space and arrange it for a more productive and collaborative environment? What are the obstacles to making this change?

Activity:

Explore your existing department floor plan. How could you create a more collaborative environment?

Time Management:

What percentage of your day is taken up with meetings? Are they collaborative, regular, productive, and necessary? How about your team members? Write down specific examples of how that time expenditure impacts productivity—positively and negatively.

How can you change the culture of the meetings to maximize the value of your team members' time while creating a collaborative environment?

Activity:

Pick one week from the past month. Chart the hours you spent to create a visual of your time in meetings. Reflect on the value of each meeting. Note the days when you feel great progress was made and the time spent in the meeting was 100% worthwhile. Note the days that were "swallowed" in meetings. What could you have done differently to protect more time to drive initiatives and revenue for your department?

Day/Hours worked	Time spent in meetings outside the department	Time spent in meeting within the department	% of time in meetings	Reflections on the level of productivity vs. time spent that day in meetings
Monday				
Tuesday				
Wednesday				
Thursday				
Friday				

Part Two: Becoming "Fearless"

Think of a specific, current example of an issue your department is facing that you know needs to change. Consider and document the "worst-case scenarios." Could these scenarios actually happen if you act fearlessly to correct specific needs for a change?

Taking that same example, how will revenue be impacted if there isn't a change? What could happen to your department? What else could be damaged if you continue the same course?

Activity:

Worst-case Scenario Exercise

Worst-case scenario	Actual scenario

Part Three: The Results-Oriented Team

It is difficult to inspire a non-revenue producing team to understand how they fit into the big picture and contribute to the organization's bottom line. How does your department track revenue as it relates to their work? How does your team fit into the big picture of your organization? What steps can you take to ensure your team members understand trackable revenue for a non-revenue producing position?

Activity:

Chart how your internal team members fit into the big picture for the team and the organization to clarify their value and spot opportunities to contribute.

Team member	Role	Contribution to revenue	Contribution to organizational goals	Opportunities to contribute

DAY TWO
Live Your PVTV

Identifying and documenting your PVTV (Purpose, Vision, Tenets, and Values) will enable you to create alignment within your team. Every successful startup has a construct that clearly states why the company is in business, what type of company it wants to become, and how it's going to achieve that goal. Most important are the Values that guide the team along the way. Your PVTV will be those guardrails to run your department like a startup.

Personal Reflection

What traits do you associate with an entrepreneur?

Think of an entrepreneur you know personally or who is well known. What traits do they possess to make them successful? What entrepreneurial traits do you possess?

Are you genuinely engaged in your team? Are you sufficiently present, intellectually and physically? Think of specific examples of how your team members witness your passion. How can you model the culture of change you want to see within your department or organization? What steps would it take to create this change?

Teamwork

Part One: PVTV

What matters most to your team? What are the guideposts that shape your culture and guide your behavior as individuals working toward a larger group objective and as a team working together?

Activity:

Understanding the PVTV (Purpose, Vision, Tenets, and Values) of your department will provide the foundation to drive the change you want to achieve. Remember, your ultimate goal is to run your department like a startup—goals driven, with a collaborative culture, and capable of making and implementing decisions with confidence and speed.

In this activity, you will create your own PVTV. Begin by writing down your Purpose statement—why do you exist? Then consider what you want the department or organization to become— your Vision. Align the steps you'll take to support those larger objectives. Create your Values last, to provide a set of lenses through which the team can assess priorities and behaviors going forward.

Crafting Your PVTV

Purpose	*Why do we exist?*	
Vision	*What do we want to become?*	
Tenets	*How are we going to do it?*	
Values	*What guides us along?*	

Part Two: Creating Ritual

What are the steps you take to get ready for the day? How do you keep track of trackable goals for the day? What is your ritual to get focused?

Activity:

What percent of your day are you giving to Headspace? How can you protect more time to be proactive about higher-level objectives, and less time reacting to "urgent" to-do items? Find a way to set aside 20% of your day to work on strategic growth and development priorities.

List three items you are working on to proactively grow the profitability of your department. What percentage of time do you currently protect to focus on these items? Look at your calendar for the coming week and block time.

Action item	Protected time

DAY THREE

Trust in the Right People

Once you have established your PVTV, understanding your team and how they fit into the vision for your department is essential. Understanding how to create a culture of recognizing wins, instilling the PVTV, and aligning your team to your goals is essential to implement The Five-Day Turnaround.

Personal Reflection

What do you call the members of your team to your peers?

What process do you engage when preparing to add an internal or external hire to your team? How do you plan your questions for interviewing to ensure you uncover whether or not the individual is likely to succeed and live out the company's PVTV?

Teamwork

What is the makeup of your team (contractors, permanent employees, a mix?) List how you tailor your communications for individual employees. How does your messaging of performance goals tend to differ? How do you get contractors to buy into your plan and PVTV, rather than their personal agenda?

What do you do to celebrate wins and team members? What is your systematic approach that proactively recognizes individuals? How are team members involved in recognizing one another?

How are you nurturing an environment of successful outcomes, instead of hours worked?

Activity:

Document specific areas of improvement that will enable you to create change in your department that supports a Five-Day Turnaround culture.

For each employee, make a list of why you hired them, the strengths you see demonstrated in their persona and work, and how these strengths support your PVTV.

How does your team match your hiring goals to implement The Five-Day Turnaround model? Where can you improve?

Employee name	Why you hired them	Strengths demonstrated	PVTV matches

DAY FOUR
Moving at the Speed of Startup

The ability as a leader to react quickly and to take advantage of business opportunities is the fourth component of The Five-Day Turnaround. Keeping focus, leading by example, embracing a minimally viable product (MVP) to increase productivity, and removing speed bumps or stumbling blocks are pillars of moving your department at the Speed of Startup.

Personal Reflection

What required meetings, processes, or sign-offs are inhibiting the speed at which your organization can move? How are they inhibiting your department?

What is your most important contribution to the organization? Where are the areas you can give your team more autonomy? How will this help them move through initiatives faster? How will this lead to more "wins" for your department?

Teamwork

How do you determine and manage your "One Thing"? Refer back to the Headspace activity on Day Two. How are you managing your schedule? How are you tracking the percentage of time you're blocking to work on your "One Thing"?

Activity:

In the context of The Five-Day Turnaround effort, MVP stands for "Minimum Viable Product." Think of a time when you and your teammates have worked tirelessly to create a product based on a corporate initiative, only to have leadership return pages and pages of edits and changes before the product or initiative can go to the customer.

How can you increase the productivity of your team by reducing the time in production until you genuinely understand the results leadership expects? What can you do in your position to ensure that your team has a clear action plan for these types of initiatives?

List current initiatives/projects and their timelines. Where can the process be sped up to present to leadership? How will this approach be received by your team members and leadership?

Initiative or project	Timeline to delivery	Hurdles to progress	Strategies to accelerate progress

DAY FIVE
Welcome Failure

Embracing failure and helping your team members grow from the failure is key to the fifth day of The Five-Day Turnaround. Your ability as a leader to implement a process to use failure as a link toward meeting your goals will change how your department responds to failure and transform it into a platform for progress.

Personal Reflection

Reflect on a time when you failed professionally.

What did you learn from that failure? How have you grown from the failure—professionally? Personally? How have your challenges impacted your confidence as a leader—negatively and positively?

Teamwork

How are you creating a culture that embraces failure? What steps do you take to help a team member understand where the process broke down and where a failure occurred? How do you coach and develop the team member to grow from the failure to ensure it is not repeated?

Activity:

Think of a team member who has had a quantifiable failure (large or small). What caused the failure? How could it have been prevented? How did you react? What steps did you take to coach the employee to resist losing confidence and to grow from the experience?

Use the exercise below to walk through an example of how to "coach out" of a failure for a team member.

Failed opportunity	*What was the failure? What was the quantitative and qualitative effect of the failure?*	
Analysis	*Where was the breakdown?* • *Direction from leadership team* • *Direction from you as a manager* • *The inability of a team member to ask for help* • *The inability of a team member to understand instructions* • *Other*	
Coaching development	*Identify the details with the team member* • *Reflect on what happened* • *Reflect on how it could have been prevented* • *Work together to glean insight from the experience* • *Determine whether the insight would benefit others* *Build an action plan for moving forward with greater ability and confidence*	
Potential growth outcomes	*Establish a time to reflect back on the plan and to highlight the team member's growth from the failure*	

How will this activity build a culture of embracing failure? How will it help you with confidence as a leader? How will it help the confidence of your team?

221

BUSINESS & LIFE HACKS

PRELUDE

Vision Casting

Make a list of the three changes you can make within your department that would make the biggest positive impact on how you work.

Confidence

Write down an entrepreneur you admire. Make a list of the qualities you share with that person, which will give you confidence as a leader.

Quick Wins

Make a list of quick wins for your department/organization. For each, identify what you need to do or who you need to know to accomplish the win.

Internal Support

Rank the decision-makers in your organization by those who are likely to be your greatest advocates. Similarly, rank the decision-makers in your organization by which are most likely to represent a hurdle to your progress. For each, note why.

Put It All Together

With your vision as the foundation, compare your three lists—areas of confidence, realistic quick wins, and internal supporters. Note which changes rise to the top of the "yes" list and which represent obstacles to creating a culture of change within your team.

DAY ONE / *Trait One / Do or Die Mindset*

The Importance of the Do or Die Mindset

Embracing the Do or Die Mindset is the first step in the process to transform the team to work as a successful startup. Ask yourself if you and your team are "all in" on your convictions. If you aren't, consider what you need to do to act with greater confidence and speed.

The Three Behaviors in the Do or Die Mindset

There are three core behaviors in the Do or Die Mindset:

1. Build an Unflinching Belief in Yourself
2. Operate with Fearlessness
3. Be Results-Oriented

Build an Unflinching Belief in Yourself

Take in the power of believing in yourself. Spend 30 minutes making a list of what you would attempt to do if you were sure you would succeed.

Operate with Fearlessness

Review all of the initiatives and campaigns you and your team are working on. Highlight the ones you are doing out of fear, and for each, create an action plan to change course immediately.

Worst-case Scenarios

Think of a specific example your team is facing that you know needs to change. Write down the worst-case scenario(s) that could happen if you act fearlessly. Delete the ones that are not actually likely. For the remaining scenarios, identify how you need to course correct.

How to Be Results-Oriented

Begin and test every effort with the question, "Are we doing this because it will achieve our biggest objective(s)?" If the answer is "no," don't do it. If the answer is "yes," build a plan and track the results.

Get Unstuck

Where is your team stuck? List specific examples. Where are processes or decisions overly cautious?

Justifying Non-Revenue Producers

Note how your department tracks revenue and how non-revenue -producing team members (or teams) fit into the "Big Picture" for your organization. List steps you can take to ensure your team members understand trackable revenue for a non-revenue-producing position.

Environment

Is your physical environment impeding or encouraging productivity? Identify opportunities to revise how you use your existing space and arrange it to be more productive. Consider the potential obstacles to making the change.

Meeting Times

Make a list of how much of your day is made up of meetings. Make a second list of how much time each day your team spends in meetings. Note which meetings help productivity and which get in the way, and adjust the schedule accordingly.

Reputation

Consider your reputation within the team and the organization. List the improvements you could make to position yourself to win over the support of your peers and decision-makers.

DAY TWO / Trait Two / PVTV

Act Like a Successful Startup

A successful startup does more than just innovate. In fact, a startup's success has more to do with how quickly they pivot to create and adopt change. A successful startup team is nimble, focused, and unified in what they're trying to achieve. In what ways does your team resemble a successful startup?

PVTV

Your PVTV is your total action plan. It is composed of four elements:

1. Purpose
2. Vision
3. Tenets
4. Values

Create Your PVTV

Gather your team leaders to create your PVTV. Write it on a whiteboard where you can discuss and share it until it's right. Work on each one until it's short, punchy, easy to recite, and memorable.

- What is your company's Purpose? (Why do we exist?)
- What is its Vision? (What do we want to become?)
- What are your key Tenets? (How will we accomplish our Purpose and Vision?)
- What Values guide the team along the journey?

Team Responsibility

For PVTV to work, your team must be fully committed to executing against the plan together. The leadership team should take responsibility for establishing the Purpose, Vision, and

Tenets, and sharing them with the rest of the team. The entire team should work together to develop the supporting Values.

Personal Responsibility

Reflect on what you can do in a leadership role to ensure that your organization's PVTV is a part of everything you and your team do for your organization.

Leadership Roles

Reflect on your leadership team. Do you have an "Eric" or a "Meredith"? List ways they work well and respond so you can involve them in creating and building support for your team's PVTV.

Operationalizing

For the PVTV to work, your team must operationalize it. The first way to do that is to start each meeting by reciting the PVTV. Memorize the guidelines word for word.

Morning Ritual

Build a Morning Ritual that sets your day on the right track. Make sure the process helps you to do three things:

1. Get organized
2. Get focused
3. Prioritize your Headspace

Building Headspace

Keep a Headspace list of your most important priorities in a format you can access from anywhere (like an Evernote app or a favorite small notebook). Organize the list with labels or hashtags so you can access your ideas quickly when you need them.

Priorities

If your Headspace list grows too long, go one by one and question which ones are truly important. Eliminate the ones that are distracting you from your most important ideas.

Regular Check-ins

Hold a mandatory all-hands meeting for a half hour at the same time every week. Make it valuable enough that people are glad to prioritize the appointment. Start with reciting PVTV and spend the time reviewing how things are aligning with the team goals.

Peer Recognition

Recognize team members who actively embody and excel at your Core Values, and whenever possible, have team members recognize one another.

Finding Your People

No matter who you are or what you're trying to accomplish, rely on a good mentor and nurture a strong network.

DAY THREE / *Trait Three* / *Trust in the Right People*

Words Matter

Think for a moment—what do you call the employees who report to you? "Team Members" are a group of individuals working together to achieve a common goal. "Resources" are people you use to achieve what you want.

Hire Against Team Values

Evaluate all of your team members against your set Values. If you believe that any of them are never going to fit in, ask them to leave and hire individuals who fit the Values you've set to support your Vision and Purpose.

Evaluate Team Members

A structured way to make hard choices about team members is to create three categories. One for "Yes" team members, one for "Yes, but needs work," and a third for "No." Put each team member in the appropriate category to get a clear sense of who works well where they are, who may need to change their role or perform differently, and who needs to be replaced.

Put the Right People, in the Right Position, at the Right Time

As you evaluate team members against team Values, be aware of The Peter Principle, which says that people keep getting promoted until they find themselves in a position not suitable for their strengths, and that's where they stay. This process can make someone go from being a reliable team member to being a detriment.

The Person or the Situation

If you evaluate team members against team Values and find that you have a team member who had been in the right position but no longer seems to fit the role, consider whether they have changed for the worse or if your environment has transformed.

Roles Exercise

Map out the organizational structure you'd create if you were starting from scratch. Rank the roles you need most, the team structure that makes the most sense, and the roles you need to change, add, or remove.

Who Trusts You

Write a list of your peers. Include your CEO. Rate them on a scale of 1-10, with 10 being "marvelous" and 1 being "terrible" in describing your relationship with them.

Don't Forget

Either during or directly following a meeting, capture your notes so you are certain you haven't missed anything.

Titles Matter

Consider your title. Does it signify the role you play—or need to play? If not, what change would tell a clearer story?

Trust

Trust is central to effectiveness and the ability of your team to get real work done.

DAY FOUR / *Trait Four* / *Move at the Speed of Startup*

Lead by Example

If you want your team to move fast, they have to see *you* moving fast. List all the ways you're acting as a bottleneck in decision-making or getting stuck in analysis paralysis, along with how you can speed up the associated effort.

Move at the Speed of Startup

Moving at the Speed of Startup requires four main behaviors. Consider how you do each of the following. Note what you do well and where you can make meaningful improvements in the following areas:

- Daily, weekly, and monthly focus
- Lead by example
- Embrace the MVP
- Remove speed bumps

Productivity at a Glance

Color code your calendar to see quickly where you're spending time each day and each week. For example, Work, Family, and Doing Good activities each have an associated color. Whenever you put something on your calendar, add it in the appropriate color.

Idea Killers

To grow fast, your team must be open to new ideas. List the "Idea Killers" that restrain innovative thinking. Share them with the team so they can replace hesitation with openness to blaze new trails.

Embrace the MVP

Use the Minimum Viable Product (MVP) approach to help your team use time more efficiently and produce work people actually want. Get an idea out as quickly as you can so you can gather immediate feedback about what works and what doesn't. Use the insight to perfect your final deliverable.

Remove Speed Bumps

What is slowing your team down? Make a list of the bottlenecks, unnecessary processes and meetings, peer relationships, and hesitations that you need to fix in order to move faster.

Revisit Client Relationships

List all the things your team is doing for a client out of fear or distrust. Take a moment to rethink the relationship—what would you do differently if you had to repitch the account? How would you structure the partnership?

The Value of the RFP

Using the insights you built as you considered a client relationship, create a "virtual" RFP to keep you thinking creatively. Present the client with fresh strategic direction, new creative executions, and better ways to monitor the relationship.

DAY FIVE / *Trait Five* / *Welcome Failure*

Take Chances and Learn from Mistakes

Consider how you "put yourself out there" as a leader and where you're held back by fear. List areas where you have a genuine unflinching belief in yourself and where you act fearlessly. Jot down the risks of failing in front of your team. Would they see you as less of a leader? Would they join you in building a culture that welcomes (purposeful) failure and thrives on trust?

Welcome Failure

A culture that welcomes purposeful failure in the process of acting fearlessly and pursuing results has four main beliefs. Write down examples of each in your team. Have they been negative or positive?

1. Fail Fast
2. Fail Often
3. Only Make New Mistakes
4. Reward Failure

The Ultimate Goal

A team that acts like a successful startup behaves in five ways. How do you grade yourself as a leader on each of these? How do you grade your team?

1. The Do or Die Mindset
2. Live Your PVTV (Purpose, Vision, Tenets, and Values)
3. Trust in the Right People
4. Move at the Speed of Startup
5. Welcome Failure

BONUS SECTION

Visit *The 5-Day Turnaround* website (www.5dayturnaround.com/bonus) for a bonus section that details a conversation between Will and Matt about optimizing the productivity and cost of team meetings, complete with useful hacks you can implement immediately in your own team space.

Be sure to check out this same section of the website to read a bonus chapter, "Friendly People," that offers additional insights into ways to create a company culture that keeps teams focused, motivated, and inspired.

ACKNOWLEDGMENTS

The phrase, "it takes a village," must have been originally said about writing a book. Something that I initially thought was a solo affair is anything but. It would be impossible for me to capture everyone who helped me through the process of writing *The 5-Day Turnaround*. To those whom I did not list below, please know I greatly appreciate you.

First, I have to acknowledge my incredible team of dragons at Dragon Army. I'm honored to be on this entrepreneurial journey with you all, and I appreciate your support as I disappeared at times in order to put pen to paper to complete this book.

To Ryan Tuttle, the mother of dragons, for being the Yin to my Yang for so many years, and for making sure we laugh along the way.

To Raj Choudhury, for giving me the honor of being your partner as we started our entrepreneurial journey together at UNC-Charlotte in 1998. I would not be who I am if not for your friendship, partnership, and great example.

To Danny Davis, for not only being the best friend a guy could have, but also for dropping out of college and working with Raj and me to build Spunlogic into a great company. And Raghu Kakarala, for taking a chance on three young kids who didn't know what they were doing. We created something special together.

To Adam Walker, for being next to me as we dreamed big (no, bigger!) dreams with 48in48, and for showing me and everyone around you that a person can put family first and still achieve greatness in business.

To Mike Popowski and Carla Guy, for reminding me what driven, passionate, and yes, competitive entrepreneurs can achieve. What you've built with Dagger over the past few years is nothing short of incredible, and you both inspire me to be a better entrepreneur.

To David Cummings, for both your friendship and support for the last 15 years. Your impact on Atlanta's entrepreneurs (and me) is nothing short of amazing.

To Dave Mathews and Jim Boykin, for teaching me not only how to swing a tennis racket, but more importantly, the necessity of a never-quit work ethic and the power of leading by example.

To the many people who gave me advice or allowed me to interview them for this book, including Paul Brown, Michael McCathren, Adam Albrecht, Gene Hammett, Mark O'Brien, and Douwe Bergsma. Your input and advice helped shape this book for the better in a million different ways.

To my friends that spend their entire lives doing the good work of helping others, including Ann Cramer, Doug Shipman, Jack Harris, Michelle Nunn, Terence Lester, Qaadirah Abdur-

Rahim, Kimberly Parker, Kemie Nix, Ashley Jones, and Jane Turner. You inspire me to be a better person.

To Charles Brewer, for showing me that a company can achieve greatness while also putting its people and culture first.

To Ken Bernhardt, for being the best mentor, friend, and role model a young entrepreneur could ask for. I'm blessed to have you in my life.

To Rachelle Kuramoto and the Watchword team, for helping me take this book across the finish line, pulling insights and ideas together in ways I never could.

To my beautiful sisters, Jennifer, Kelly, and Joanna, for helping push this over the finish line with your copious notes and critical edits (and supportive words!). And to Dorothy Miller-Farleo (a.k.a. DMF), who stepped in at the end and wrestled this book out the door with us!

To Jessica Carruth, for your always positive and reassuring words, your steadfast dedication to making sure we achieved excellence while also hitting our aggressive deadlines, and for constantly reassuring me that "it's going to happen!" As usual, you were right.

To Stan Rapp, for believing in me and inspiring me to achieve more than I ever thought I could. You are one of the best people I know, and I look up to you with great admiration.

To my wife's parents, Charlie and Peg Richards, for welcoming me into your incredible family and for raising the most wonderful person in the world. To my dad, for showing me how hard and how rewarding entrepreneurship can be, and to my mom for being there for my siblings and me—always. Your positivity and kindness light up all of us.

And most of all to my wife, Emily, and our amazing children, for supporting me on all the crazy journeys we take together. Your encouragement and belief in me keeps me going.